In working with Ian Broc
be a person with a unique
process. He constantly cl
perceived to be unlocking the full potential of an organisation or
delivering superior value to the customer.
Anyone who embraces the philosophies Ian promotes in this book
will have a competitive advantage in an increasingly customer-
driven marketplace.

Ian Hendry,
Joint Managing Director, Sovereign Assurance

Regardless of where you sit in the company hierarchy, the messages
embodied in these chapters will give you 'the edge'
to succeed

Peter Rasmussen,
Executive Officer, Employers' and Manufacturers' Association

The cornerstones of any business are product quality, low cost and
customer value. To be truly successful, businesses need to excel in at
least one of these and be very good in the other two. *Second To None*
is a wonderful insight for those companies who cannot achieve the
world's lowest cost or highest quality, but want to maintain a competitive advantage. It is also a practical guide to assist businesses identify
their strengths and weaknesses in delivering customer value.

Oscar Gregory,
General Manager Primary Operations, BHP New Zealand

Dr Ian Brooks is one of New Zealand's leading business speakers. He
is passionate about business development and his message is
relevant, tailored to the client's brief and up-to-date. Our clients
constantly rate Ian as an excellent speaker.

Debbie Tawse,
Managing Director, Celebrity Speakers (NZ) Ltd

Second To None is a succinct distillation of many texts and comments
on customer focus. . . and includes a number of challenging questions
to test how you are performing. . . an excellent, actionable book for
those who are seroius about inplementing successful customer-oriented
strategies in the increasingly competitive global marketplace.

Bob Heywood
Managing Director, Challenge Realty Group

In *Second To None*, Ian Brooks presents us with six extremely powerful strategies which, if followed, will ensure it will be your business that survives rather than your competitors. A very compelling argument.

Wayne Holmes
Managing Director, Holmes Packaging

. . . a hard-hitting, practical book which makes excellent reading for all those in management . . . backed up with practical examples . . . structured in a way which makes it easy to read.

Reg Garters
General Manager, NZIM, Christchurch

Ian brooks is a refreshing, innovative thinker who adds value to the businesses he is associated with . . . His focus on people, customers and processes zeroes in on the basic elements for business success. *Second To None* will become essential reading for business people throughout Australasia.

Grant Carruthers
Director, Westco Lagan Limited

Dr Brooks' book draws an accurate picture of global competition, provides real-life case studies and effective strategies for figuring out what your customers may want — and how to give it to them.

Caroll du Chateau
former editor, *Management Magazine*

Ian Brooks provides extremely powerful guidance for success in business with his new book *Second To None* . . . with great clarity . . . a sure catalyst for action and success.

Norman Fitzgerald
Medical Director, Southern Community Laboratories Ltd

Customers demand value. This book outlines simple, sound and decisive strategies for creating value . . . compelling reading for those serious about competing in the nineties and beyond.

Dennis Jones
Managing Director, TPF Restaurants, Burger King NZ

The customer might not always be right, but he's your lifeblood. This book explains how to make and keep customers in a practical way.

Selwyn Parker
journalist and author

SECOND TO NONE

Dr Ian Brooks is one of New Zealand's leading business consultants. For nearly twenty-five years, Ian has worked with companies in New Zealand, Australia, Canada, and Fiji helping them to improve their business performance. His consulting firm, Brooks Royston, with partners Julie Rowlands and Wayne Morris, is recognised for its expertise in quality management, organisational change and staff training. Together, their clients have included large corporations such as Air New Zealand, Auckland City Council, Carter Holt Harvey, CSR, Kiwi Dairy, New Zealand Post, Tasman Pulp and Paper and Shell New Zealand; government departments such as Civil Aviation and Revenue Canada; and medium to small businesses such as Challenge Realty, Holmes Packaging, Lion Breweries, Methanex, Progressive Meats and New Zealand Sugar.

Ian has worked in nearly every sector of the economy from district councils, law firms and radio stations through to retail businesses, banks and insurance companies, dairy companies, meat processing plants and forestry ventures. As well as having considerable consulting experience, Ian has had many years of practical business management. He is currently a company director sitting on the boards of Caledonian Financial Services and Nahanni Publishing Ltd.

A much sought after speaker, Ian delivers over 100 seminars and keynote addresses at national and international conferences each year. He has a reputation for being able to communicate effectively to all business people from the boardroom to the factory floor. Ian helps people to understand the elements of business success and has practical suggestions for how they can be implemented. His audiences are inspired by his powerful message, entertained by his presentation and motivated by his enthusiasm. Most importantly, they treasure what they have learned.

Nearly five thousand copies of Ian's first book, *The Yellow Brick Road: The Path to Building a Quality Business in New Zealand,* have been sold since its release in October of 1995. It continues to sell strongly. Ian is the editor of the *Brooks Royston Business Report,* a twelve-page monthly digest containing stimulating ideas, useful information and practical business tips drawn from Ian's own writing and from business publications around the world. Ian has produced four audio tapes: *Doing Business in the Nineties — It's Tough But It Ain't Complicated,* outlines four keys to running a successful business. *The Art of Creating Value* summarises the six strategies for becoming number one in your market discussed in this book. In *Become A Changemaker,* Ian outlines seven principles for bringing about organisational change. His fourth tape, called *It's Gotta Be You,* is a motivational tape full of ideas about how you can reach your full potential.

A recognized business educator, Ian is a founding member of the New Zealand Quality College and is a member of the faculty of the Advanced Management Programme organised by the New Zealand Institute of Management in Christchurch.

Since 1982, Ian has lived with his wife, Deb, and their three sons, Kent, Chris and Matt, on Auckland's North Shore.

There are two kinds of companies:
those that compete and those that are closed.

SECOND
TO
NONE

6 Strategies
for Creating
Superior
Customer
Value

Ian Brooks

Nahanni Business
An Imprint of Nahanni Publishing Limited
Auckland, New Zealand

First published 1997 Nahanni Business
An Imprint of Nahanni Publishing Limited,
Auckland, New Zealand, 1997
Tel. (09) 479 3330   Fax. (09) 479 3354

ISBN 0 9583506 1 2

Production by Pages Literary Pursuits
Printed by Wright & Carman (NZ) Limited, Wellington

Dedication

To my wife, Deb, and our three sons, Kent, Chris and Matt.
Thank you for your love, understanding and support, not only
in this project, but in all the work I have thrown myself into
over the years.

Acknowledgements

A book does not get written without the assistance of many others: *Second To None* is no exception. I am indebted to the following people for finding the time in their very busy schedules to give me the benefits of their expertise and wisdom.

To my friend and business partner, Tom Smith of Marketing Vision, for his guidance, support and practical assistance with this project. Your hard work and valuable counsel have helped this book through every stage of its development.

To my friends, Dr John Burman and his wife Kay, who have spent many hours reviewing the various drafts of the manuscript. Thank you for having the courage to give me an honest assessment of my work.

To my friends and business colleagues, Howard Russell of Strategic Insight and David Anderson of Sovereign Assurance, for taking the time to review the manuscript. You have both made very valuable suggestions which have improved this book.

To Debbie Tawse at Celebrity Speakers (NZ) Ltd for her encouragement, advice and support in taking this book into the marketplace. Thank you, too, for doing such an excellent job of representing me.

To Chris O'Brien of Pages Literary Pursuits, for transforming a sheaf of papers into an attractive and readable book.

Dr. Ian Brooks
Auckland, New Zealand
September, 1997

Contents

✸ Introduction

✸ Strategy 1

✸ Strategy 2

✸ Strategy 3

✳ Strategy 4

✳ Strategy 5

✺ Strategy 6

✺ Beginning The Journey

✺ Epilogue

✸ In The Beginning

In the beginning was the customer. The leader of the Business People saw the unfulfilled need and met it.

And it was good.

Others from the Tribe of Customers saw the benefits that could be gotten from the Business Leader. They flocked to his house as the sparrows come to the newly sown field.

And it was even better.

The Business Leader began to enjoy the fruits of his commerce. Since there was custom aplenty, there was no need to labour so hard. Besides, the Customers were so unreasonable.

But others belonging to the Business People watched. They saw their leader turn a blind eye to his customers' needs. They attacked his weak flank and plundered his business.

A plague had descended on the house of the Business Leader. There was weeping and wailing and gnashing of teeth.

It was a time of remorse and re-engineering.

And thus it was that the Business Consultant was born into this world.

> Reprinted without permission from the
> *Book of Consultants*, Chapter 1, verses 1–6

 Introduction

The Foundation

> Business today is tough. It is a crowded marketplace full of very sophisticated and demanding customers. Profit margins are being squeezed and nearly all products and services have been reduced to being commodity items. Nevertheless, business is still the most powerful vehicle for improving the quality of life for all people — be they customers, staff, suppliers, shareholders or just people who live in the same town.
>
> If your goal is to be second to none, you must compete on value. You should aim to provide so much value that people will be disappointed if they cannot do business with you. Create value for your customers, staff and for the residents of your community, and you will create value for yourself. If these people win, you will win.
>
> Knowing what to do, of course, is the easy bit. The trick is knowing how to do it. That is what this book is all about. It sets out six powerful strategies you can use to become number one in your market.

Business: The Art Of Creating Value

I have learned two things about business in the past ten years:

1. Everyone believes their business is unique.
2. Everyone is wrong!

I know it is easy to believe that *your* business is different. Perhaps you have an unusual product, or a special process for manufacturing. Perhaps you have a monopoly due to government regulation, or maybe you trade with a unique sector of the market. But fundamentally every business is the same because the business of every business is creating value. Customers do not want your products and services, they want

> *Businesses do not so much make products and services as they buy customers by producing things that customers value.*

what your products and services can do for them. They do not want to know what you have to do to produce those products and services. They are not interested in the features of your products and they do not want service. They want value. Think of it this way: businesses do not so much make products and services as they buy customers by producing things that customers value. Harley-Davidson, for example, does not think of itself as selling motorcycles but as offering "a lifestyle, an experience, fun."

Business is the activity of creating value. Those who understand this best will succeed. Those who do not, will struggle.

Business Is Tough

> *"Give me a Coke, please."*
> *"Would you like a Classic Coke, a New Coke, a Diet Coke or a Cherry Coke?"*
> *"I'd like a Diet Coke, please."*
> *"Would you like a regular Diet Coke or a caffeine-free Diet Coke?"*
> *"To hell with it. Give me a ginger ale."*

Millions of people own businesses throughout the world, and hundreds of millions more rely on those businesses for their livelihood. Right now, most of these people are feeling nervous — and so they should, because business is tough. In 1995, more than 4000 retailers shut their doors in the United States alone and the death toll was expected to climb by another 7000 in 1996.

Business is tough because today people are trying to win in a crowded and competitive marketplace, where customers have choices they never had before. If customers want pizza for dinner, they can make one (from scratch or with a mix), buy one from the grocery store (frozen or fresh), order one from the local pizzeria (eat-in or takeaway) or get one from their local petrol station or convenience store. Customers have so many choices because it is a global marketplace. Thanks to modern technology and freer world trade, customers do not have to settle for the best in town anymore — they can get the best in the world. They also have more choices because the boundaries between industries are becoming blurred. Insurance companies sell mortgage and investment products, and banks sell insurance. The Canadian Imperial Bank of Commerce hopes to generate Can$500 million in insurance premiums by 1998 and has applied for membership of the Canadian Life and Health Insurance Association. Petrol stations sell groceries and in many countries food stores are selling petrol. In Britain, 25 per cent of all petrol is sold by grocery stores and in France the figure is 50 per cent. In Australia, the grocery chain Woolworths has recently entered the retail petrol market, and it will not be long before a similar company does the same thing in New Zealand. On the other hand, in the USA gas stations earn 40 per cent of their revenue from non-petroleum products such as tobacco and beverages.

The Internet allows shoppers to browse the markets of the world without leaving home. There is now an Internet shopping mall in Auckland with a full grocery store. Browse the aisles with your PC, fill your electronic shopping basket with delicious goodies, go through the electronic checkout and wait for the groceries to be delivered to your home. If shoppers do not want to go to the trouble of searching the Internet themselves, there are companies they can e-mail who will find what they are looking for and have it shipped to them within 24 hours.

Because they have so many choices, most customers see everything as a commodity. Recently, I heard a senior vice-president of one of the world's largest companies tell an audience of law students: "You're not going to like hearing this, but the law is a commodity. We have lots of excellent law firms to choose from." Even the most sophisticated products have become commodity items and nearly all producers are finding profit margins falling as a result.

Not only is today's marketplace crowded with competitors, it is full of demanding customers who want everything for free by yesterday. These customers shop with confidence because they know, as you know, that they have the power. Over the past fifteen years there has been a major shift in power in our society — not political or military power, but economic power. And this power has gone to the consumer.

Today's customers are better educated and more sophisticated than in the past. They are less forgiving, less tolerant and less loyal as a result. Excuses do not cut it with these customers. They want performance. It is these customers who dictate product quality, service standards and prices. They know they can fire anyone in the company from the CEO on down simply by withdrawing their business. And, they are prepared to do it.

You could become a dinosaur much more quickly today than a decade ago. That's the real fear we all have. Whether it's a Microsoft, whether it's a mutual-fund company offering chequing on its accounts, they could take a great deal of our business away if we are not nimble.

Charles Baillie, CEO
Toronto Dominion Bank

5

In spite of the tough competition and the demanding customers, I am very positive about business because business creates winners. Private enterprise, more than government, has the potential to improve the quality of life for everyone. Conducted properly, business creates winners out of:

- **customers** who get the value they are seeking;
- **staff** who get rewarded for creating that value;
- **suppliers** who deliver the raw materials you need;
- the **community** which sees jobs created and services provided, all by a company which cares about the environment and the people living in it;
- **shareholders** who receive a good return on their investment;
- even **competitors** benefit because they are forced to get better just to survive.

Succeeding In Business

Lots of people given advice about how to win in a tough marketplace. John Paul Getty, the oil billionaire, said that to succeed in business you must do three things:

1. rise early;
2. work late;
3. discover oil.

Assuming you have not discovered much oil lately, you will have to turn to Plan B which says that business success comes from hard work and perseverance.

It Takes Some Special Work

Bill Gates once said: "Profit is not a natural condition. It takes some special work to create." Being the world's richest commoner, he should know.

That special work, of course, is creating value for your customers. Successful business people do not just think about creating value, they are passionate about it. They have a vision about how their business can, in some small way, make the world a better place for their customers. Those who aim to be number one dedicate themselves to solving their customers'

Our Changing World

Telecommunications

"In the time-honoured way of trade diplomacy, 69 members of the World Trade Organisation reached a last-minute deal to open their telecom markets to competition and foreign investment, and agreed to observe common principles of telecoms' regulation. Together the signatories account for more than 90 per cent of global telecom revenues of US$ 660 billion. Liberalisation is expected to lead to lower telecom prices around the world."

The Economist, February 22, 1997

problems and to making life easier for them. They get excited about discovering new ways to improve the quality of their customers' lives.

Successful business leaders also know that the only person who can determine whether all the hard work and skills have produced value is their customer. Your customers will define your business for you. They will tell you what to sell, how you should present it to the market and what changes would add even more value. Your customers will tell you whether you are different from your competitors and how.

It has to do with passion. Not just doing something because it will make you successful, but because you believe — with true entrepreneurial fervour — in making life better for your customer.

Marketing Guru, Stan Rapp

Basically, your customers will tell you everything you need to know to run a successful business. It is just a matter of listening to them. Listen to the questions they ask, the comments they make, the objections they raise and, if you are lucky enough to hear them, to the complaints they make. Businesses serious about creating value begin by focusing on their customers.

Create Value For Your Staff

But creating value for your customers is only one ingredient for business success. If you are to succeed, those who work in your business with you must feel they, too, are getting value from your business. Turn your employees into winners.

One day I was chatting to a senior manager. "You know, Ian, I think you've got it backwards. This idea about putting your customers first is good but don't you think we ought to put our staff first. If we don't look after them, they won't want to look after the customer."

Your staff are your customers.

He has a good point. Indeed, a number of very successful CEOs, such as Herb Kellagher of Southwest Airlines, share this view. But what is a "customer"? A customer is someone who uses the products or services we produce. So, according to this definition, the primary customers of business owners and senior managers are their staff who use the instructions, policies, systems and equipment that they produce. There is no conflict between the ideas of putting your customers first and looking after your staff because your staff *are* your customers. My colleague is right. You must look after your employees because your staff will treat their customers the way they believe you treat them.

Your staff will treat their customers the way you treat them.

Do not ignore the fact that your employees also want to receive value. If they are going to work to make your business successful, there has to be something in it for them. Fair and adequate compensation is essential, but there are also other aspects of value important to staff, such as meaningful work, recognition of achievement and the opportunity for personal growth. Astute business leaders endeavour to get to know their employees and to understand their needs. They also survey employee satisfaction as frequently as they survey their paying customers. They understand that their company's ability to compete flows from the firm's culture, values, management style and reward systems. They work hard to create an environment which encourages their people to work together in teams, to operate efficient processes to create value for their customers.

Create Value For The Community

Residents of the wider community also expect to receive value from your business. In return for providing you with the opportunity to gain financial success, they expect you to protect the environment, create employment, contribute to social causes and generally operate in an ethical manner. Today, businesses are responding to this demand.

"There is just more awareness generally of what is appropriate," says James Hunter, who heads the ethics practice at KMPG in Toronto (Canada). According to Hunter, "Corporations are responsible not only to shareholders but to a larger audience, so they want to do the right thing and be seen to do the right thing."

Society is sending a very clear message to business people: Be a safe employer, be environmentally friendly, be socially responsible and give something back to the community in which you operate.

Create Value For Your Shareholders

Shareholders, of course, want value too. But they do not just want profit — although many CEOs behave as if short-term profits were the only target worth thinking about. Shareholders want the increased value that comes from growing the company's assets. Profit is just one means of creating this value. We all know that short-term profitability at the expense of sustainable growth can be disastrous.

Experienced shareholders also realize that value will come to them *after* it has been produced for the other key stakeholders: customers, staff and the community. Even for small business owners, shareholder value is the result, not the cause, of running a successful business. Professor Jon Goodman, Director of the Entrepreneurial Programme at the University

First you must satisfy the needs of the market, then you earn the profit. When you put the profit requirement first, you have the wrong strategy. The marketing decision is always made before the financial decision. It is done successfully no other way.

Winning the Marketing War

Society is sending a very clear message to business people: Be a safe employer, be environmentally friendly, be socially responsible and give something back to the community.

of Southern California, says, "I've worked with hundreds of entrepreneurs and I've never met one who said, 'I want to get rich,' who did. The successful ones say, 'I want to find a way to do animation faster,' or 'I'm really interested in adhesion.'"

J.C. Hall, the founder of Hallmark Cards which has 44 per cent market share and produces 11 million cards a day in 13,000 different designs, agrees: "If a man goes into business with only the idea of making money, chances are he won't. But if he puts service and quality first, the money will take care of itself. Producing a first class product for which there is a real need is a much stronger motivation for success than getting rich."

Strategies For Creating Value

Knowing *what* to do, of course, is the easy bit. The real trick is in learning *how* to do it. Over the years, I have been impressed by the hundreds of articles saying that if you are competing to win you must provide better customer value than anyone else. But there is not a lot of practical information about how to do that.

That is what this book is about. The next six sections outline some strategies you can employ to increase the value you create for your customers and to improve your competitive advantage. These strategies can be used by one-person businesses, 'mom and pop' businesses, small owner-operated companies, medium-sized businesses, large corporations and even government departments. They can be used singly or in combination. The more of them you use, of course, the greater your chances of becoming second to none.

If you want to be second to none create an environment which encourages your people to work together in teams to operate efficient processes to create value for your customers.

But Will They Work?

Just knowing about strategies for creating value is not enough. To be number one you must actually *do* something, change something, behave differently. In short, you must act.

Will these strategies work? Will they help you to grow your business? That is up to you. At some point you will put this book down and decide either to make these strategies work for you, or to continue with business as usual. There is no middle ground. If you cannot choose to act, you have chosen not to act. In that case, your future will be no better than your past and probably worse since the marketplace is becoming more demanding.

What worked for you last year can be your death this year. If you do not change, you will demonstrate "the triumph of hope over experience," as Dr Samuel Johnson, the English man of letters, once said of people who marry for the second time.

Read about these strategies and adapt them to your particular situation. But most importantly, act. One idea that is actually implemented is better than five that are only thought about. As Percy Barnevik, former Chairman of Asea Brown Boveri, says: "We don't need any more bright ideas. In business, success is 5 per cent strategy, 95 per cent execution."

Take a chance. Business is a four letter word spelled RISK.

Besides, in a global marketplace full of sophisticated customers who are demanding increasing value, what choice do you have?

From Tokyo to Sao Paulo to Paris, what is occurring is nothing short of a global Value Revolution. The emerging reality is that buyers... can have it all: high quality, excellent service, and competitive prices...

Robert Tucker *Win the Value Revolution*

How Are *You* Doing?

What would your staff say your business
is all about?

Which new competitors do you have now who were
not on the scene a few years ago?

Who could become your competitors in the future?

What are your customers demanding today that they
did not demand a few years ago?

What are they likely to be demanding in the future?

Do you follow the principle: If you win, I win?

Would your staff and customers agree?

If not, how would they describe the principle you do work on?

What value do you create for your staff?

For the community in which you live?

For yourself and your shareholders?

For your suppliers?

Becoming Second To None

Six Strategies for Being Number One in Your Market by Creating Superior Customer Value

Strategy **Focus On Value**

1
If business is the art of creating value, then everyone in your business must understand the concept of value and everything you do must be directed towards creating value in the eyes of your customers.

Strategy **Compete On Value, Not Price**

2
Resist the temptation to compete on the basis of price alone. It is an inadequate strategy at best and a suicidal path for both you and your competitors at worst.

Strategy **Look Through Your Customer's Eyes**

3
Since value exists only in the eyes of your customer, you must learn to see the world through your customer's eyes. Most companies do not.

Strategy **Make Your Customers Successful**

4
In this tough marketplace servicing or even satisfying your customers is not enough. Studies show that even happy customers switch to another supplier at a very high rate.

Strategy **Reduce The Costs**

5
To compete and win in this crowded market, you need to be a low-cost supplier, but instead of reducing your price, try to reduce the other four main costs that customers pay to obtain your products and services.

Strategy **Give Them Something Extra**

6
In addition to lowering the costs, increase the benefits you offer your customers. Give them something extra — at no extra charge — and delight them.

 Strategy 1

Focus On Value

The more you understand about value, the more successful you will be. The first strategy to becoming second to none in your market is to focus on creating value. Make sure each person understands value and devotes their time and energy to creating it.

Value is subjective and can be defined only by the customer. It varies not only from person to person but from one gender to the other, from time to time and from situation to situation. What any given customer will value is hard to predict specifically, but the general formula for value is benefit minus cost as judged by your customer. Customers will consider they have received value if they believe that the benefits they have received from your product or service outweigh the costs of obtaining it. Benefits are simply those features of your product or service which your customers believe will solve their problems. There are a number of costs involved in getting those benefits, however, with price being only one factor. Cost of use, and the effort, time and exposure to risk are significant factors from the customer's point of view. Many customers find these costs to be less affordable than the purchase price.

The Main Thing

Most business people work very hard but not always at the things that matter most. Internal administrative matters and crises with staff, customers, banks and suppliers consume huge amounts of time and are generally unproductive as far as customers are concerned.

The first strategy of creating superior value simply involves making sure that the focus of everything you do is to create value for your customers. When you build a relationship with

If you have chosen to work in business, you have chosen the creation of value to be your profession.

a customer, use it to learn more about how you can increase benefits. When you implement quality systems or other approaches to improving efficiency, do so to eliminate costs such as time, effort and unreliability. When you hire people, train them and build them into teams to enhance the value you create.

To succeed in business you must understand not only what you are doing, but why you are doing it. What is the purpose of your business — its reason for being? What would your customers say? Do not confuse purpose with goals and business strategy. A purpose is long-lasting because it is never fully attainable. It is something you can spend 100 years working towards and still not get there. Knowing your purpose is not a frivolous issue. Research shows that those businesses which last, such as 3M, Hewlett-Packard and Sony, each have a clearly defined purpose that has not changed since the company was founded. What is more, these purposes have described the contribution — or value — the business was going to provide to the people living in its community.

Each and every person in your business should worry about whether they are creating value because your customers worry about that constantly.

To become number one in your market, your entire staff must see that the purpose of your business is to enhance the lives of your customers. Perhaps your staff would rather not think about this. Maybe it is all a bit too much. Help them to understand that you must all worry about the contribution you make to peoples' lives, because that is all *they* — your customers — worry about. It is what they pay you to do. Every time customers make a purchase they ask themselves:

"Am I getting value for money here?"

If the answer is yes, they go away happy and are likely to return. If the answer is no, they will look elsewhere. Help your people to see that in this crowded marketplace your customers have lots of other choices. There is no eleventh commandment that says they must buy from you.

Since you have chosen to work in the world of commerce, then all of you have chosen the creation of value to be your profession. The more you understand the concept of value and how to create it, the more successful you will be. It is not easy to do but, hey, this is your job. It is what you do.

Value Is Subjective

Value is subjective. It can be determined only by the person getting it — in this case, the customer. Value does not come from the products or services you provide but from what your customers believe your products and services *can do for them.* Quality is what we build in to our products and services, value is what the customers take out. Or rather, what your customers believe they take out. When it comes to business, perception is everything. Not only must there be real value, but customers must see it. A telecommunications company in Australia put on a big drive to attract customers away from their main competitor. The key device to lure customers away was the guarantee of cheaper prices. The promotion was very successful

I've been in this business for 33 years, and it seems that every decade we get reminded of what this business is all about — providing better value to consumers.

John Pepper, CEO
Proctor & Gamble

What Is Your Purpose?

Do you know the purpose of your business — its reason for being? What is the contribution — or value — your business provides your customers and to the people living in your community?

Sony, for example, has as its purpose to "experience the joy of advancing and applying technology for the benefit of the public". Similarly, Hewlett-Packard set out to "make technical contributions for the advancement and welfare of the community" and 3M aims to "solve unsolved problems innovatively". Mary Kay Cosmetics set its sights on giving unlimited opportunity to women, and Henry Ford strove to democratize the automobile. Sam Walton built Wal-Mart to give ordinary folk the chance to buy the same things as rich people, Walt Disney was driven to make people happy, and Merck, the drug company, aspires to preserve and improve human life.

So what drives you and your company? Why does your business exist?

If you do not already know your purpose, you must discover it. I say discover because you do not create a purpose, it exists within the company already.

One advantage of knowing your purpose — or put another way, the value that you create for your customers — is that it helps you to see your business from your customer's point of view. Another is that it may open up opportunities you might not have otherwise seen. If a camera company had believed its purpose was to build better still cameras it might have missed expanding into movies, videos and photo CDs. Also, knowing the business's reason for being gives staff a noble goal to work towards.

Discover the purpose for your business. If everyone in your company knows the purpose, they will be more focused, more motivated and more successful.

And so will you.

but research later suggested that many people were back with their original supplier within twelve months. The attractiveness of cheaper prices waned when people found it hard to see that they were saving money. That is not to say they were not getting the promised savings. It is just that they could not see they were better off so they returned to the company they had always dealt with.

Previous experience is also a factor in how customers judge value. Based on their life's experience, people have clear ideas about what the product or service they are about to buy will look like, how it will work, how it will be delivered and how much it will cost. These ideas make up their expectations and they, too, differ from person to person. Some people are concerned about only price and want to know the bottom line. Others are more concerned with getting lots of detail about the benefits a product has to offer and the costs involved in purchasing and using it. Yet others appreciate most the relationship they have with the seller. Then there are those people who do not like change and who, therefore, seek products and services that suggest stability and old-fashioned ways.

Marketers would like to be able to classify consumers according to their preferences and some interesting work has been done in this area. One approach has identified at least four *styles* of customers, each perceiving value in a different way. *Achievers,* for example, strive to do well and choose those products and services that show the world how successful they are. They buy prestige items such as Rolex watches and European luxury cars. *Emulators,* on the other hand, have not been so successful but they would like to convince the world — and probably themselves — that they are. They buy Japanese sports cars and copies of expensive brands. Then there are *Family* people. They purchase products and services that help them look after their family. They purchase good, solid sedans, stationwagons and mini-vans. The *Socially Conscious* consumer supports companies that worry about the environment and people. They buy Ben and Jerry ice cream, cosmetics from the Body Shop and talk about electric cars.

Remember, when it comes to judging value your view is unimportant at best and dangerously misleading at worst. Many

I walked into an auto parts store and told the guy I wanted a windshield wiper for my Lada. He said, "That sounds like a fair exchange to me."

corporations have found their business strategy has failed because it was developed by senior managers and consultants far removed from the marketplace.

Value Is Variable

Value is not only subjective, it is highly variable. The perception changes from customer to customer, from situation to situation, and from time to time. As we all know, there are gender differences that affect purchasing decisions. A joint study by

Name That Customer

Five new groups of customers have been identified by New York marketers Yankelovich Skelly & White/Clancy Schulman based on their attitudes towards shopping, value and quality.

Strict Loyalists

These are comparison shoppers who stress quality and recognize differences between brands. They rarely give in to impulse buying but will pay a premium.

Grasshoppers

These tend to be female, single, younger and better-educated. These are the risk-takers who do not wait for sales and they don't spend their time comparison shopping. They buy what they want, but price is a key concern.

Image Makers

These are generally male, young and single, but with less education and lower incomes than Grasshoppers. This group expresses status and prestige in material terms and prizes national brand names.

Anxious Managers

These are mostly female and full-time workers with a high proportion of executives and professionals. This group values information and shows a strong preference for brands. On the other hand, they are careful shoppers.

Conservatives

Mostly male, older and retired, these people are not active shoppers. When they do shop, they like stores with knowledgeable staff. They are very loyal.

Profit Magazine, October 1991

the Chatelaine Consumer Council on Women and the automotive industry found that although both men and women seek dependability in a car, women tend to rank safety higher than men. Men, on the other hand, rate appearance, styling, horsepower and acceleration as being more important.

Not only does the idea of value vary from person to person, it can vary from one situation to another for the same person. Someone might find that a desk for their home office that cost less but required "some assembly" appealed on an occasion when they had time to spare, but not when they were busy and needed the desk quickly. This effect is most pronounced as people move through different stages of their lives. Young married couples who do not have much money are often attracted to the low-cost kit-set desk, but middle-aged parents of teenagers will usually opt to buy the pre-assembled desk. Hence, an understanding of demographics is important. Says Canadian economist and demographer David Foot: "Demographics explain about two-thirds of everything."

Baby boomers are growing older. The teenyboppers who once swept white bucks, pony tails and Frank Sinatra out of the market-place are now using their consumer power to change the way financial organisations deliver their services. Under such pressure, tomorrow's financial-services industry will bear as much resemblance to today's as Snoop Doggy Dogg does to Tommy Dorsey.
Canadian Banker,
January 1997

Business leaders who ignore demographics and their effect on what people seek will, according to Foot, likely find themselves out of business.

The customer's view also varies throughout the purchase and product use cycle. For instance, their view of value at the time of the initial purchase may be quite different from their view when making a repeat purchase. Before the purchase, the attraction comes from what the customer anticipates receiving; afterwards it comes from what they have actually experienced. As customers become more knowledgeable about the products or services available, they become more sophisticated and they become more demanding as a result.

Factors Affecting Your Customer's View Of Value

1. What they hear from other customers.

2. The urgency of the situation.

3. Past experience with a competitor or with other suppliers.

4. What they see or hear through advertising and media reports.

It Seemed Like A Good Idea

A number of years ago, telecommunications companies saw the increasing usage in cellphones and became worried that in the near future there would be a shortfall in their capacity to meet the demand.

On the advice of their experts, the telecommunications companies developed a new digital technology to handle the expected demand. After investing hundreds of millions of dollars, they launched the new product to their customers.

There were few takers.

Customers wanted to know why they should change. They wanted to see increased benefits in return for the cost of switching. Basically, they were quite content with the existing service because their phones worked just fine.

Today, telecommunications companies have to develop new features to make the digital technology look attractive. And, they will probably have to reduce the price as well.

Too bad they didn't go to their customers in the first place to discover what they would value in a cellphone.

Value Is Hard To Predict

Because there are so many subjective factors and unknowns in the equation, what the consumer will perceive as value can never be determined beforehand with any certainty. The high failure rate of new products and services shows just how difficult it is to predict what customers will purchase. The Edsel and the introduction of New Coke are classic examples. Similarly, the unforeseen success of many new products people said would never fly demonstrates how little we know about consumer psychology.

In the face of this poor track record some business gurus advise against trying to predict the market's reaction to a new product or service. Just invent new ones, they say, and try them out. If you launch enough, one or two are bound to succeed. It is just a numbers game, a matter of probability.

This is a short-sighted view. Sure, understanding what your customers value is hard to do, but that is good news. It means that if you can do this difficult job better than your rival, you

As customers become more knowledgeable about the products or services available, they become more sophisticated about the value they want and they become more demanding as customers.

The high failure rate of new products and services shows just how difficult it is to predict what customers will value.

will have a competitive advantage. In any event, it is not quite a black box. There are some guidelines to follow.

Value Is Benefit Minus Cost

Value can be expressed as a simple formula:

Value = Benefit – Cost.

As long as your customers consider the benefits they receive to be greater than the costs they pay, they will believe they have received value. Like most simple ideas, this formula is very powerful. If you adopt it as your driving principle it will help you become number one in your market. It will tell you where you are going wrong. If your customers are complaining about your costs, chances are you are not marketing your benefits very well. Many businesses, especially professional practices, fall into this trap. They give their customers detailed accounts with long lists of charges and do little to point

Two Thirds Of Everything

"Demography, the study of human populations, is the most powerful — and most underutilized — tool we have to understand the past and to foretell the future. Demographics affect everyone of us as individuals, far more than most of us have ever imagined. They also play a vital role in the economic and social life of our country...

"Demographics explain about two-thirds of everything. They tell us a great deal about which products will be in demand in five years, and they accurately predict school enrolments many years in advance. They allow us to forecast which drugs will be in fashion ten years down the road, as well as what sorts of crimes will be on the increase. They help us to know when houses will go up in value, and when they will go down...

"Demographics are critically important for business. They probably won't alter a company's financial results from one financial quarter to the next. But the management of a business that fails to pay attention to demographics for five years may wake up to find itself in a different business than it thought it was in — or not in business at all."

David Foot *Boom, Bust & Echo*

out the benefits the customer has received. A friend of mine experienced this when he went to buy a new car. He had just been appointed CEO and was choosing the company car that was part of his remuneration package. He looked at one car for NZ$65,000 and was told that if he wanted a stereo radio-cassette player it would cost $400 more. For some reason he did not buy the car.

This formula will also help you to understand why some promotional programmes work and others fail. The benefit from frequent flyer programmes is seen as being worth the cost, so they appeal to customers. On the other hand, other frequent usage programmes, such as eating at a particular restaurant, often do not seem to be worth the trouble. New versions of frequent usage programmes, such as *Air Miles* in Canada and *Fly Buys*. in New Zealand and Australia, allow customers to collect points from a wide variety of businesses. Consequently, they have been perceived by consumers as creating better value and are extremely popular. They have given the companies involved a major competitive advantage as a result.

If you aim to be second to none, your products and services must be seen by your customers to contain more value than those of your competitor's. The formula, value = benefits − costs, shows you that to increase the value you offer you must:

1. increase the benefits you offer (Strategy 6)
2. decrease the costs you charge (Strategy 5)
3. do both 1 and 2

Features are what go into your products and services. Benefits are what your customers get out of them.

Benefits Versus Features

There are two ways of looking at your product or service. One way is to see it as being full of features and the other is to see it as a bundle of benefits. Successful business people advertise benefits, set their prices on the basis of benefits and sell on the basis of benefits. More than 100 years ago, George Eastman understood that he was not selling Kodak cameras, but giving people a chance to take photographs without having to understand photography. His slogan, *You push the button, we do the rest,* launched a company that today is the fourth most powerful brand in the world.

Features are the attributes that make up the product or service, and they may be tangible or intangible. Some of the features of a coffee mug, for example, are its size, colour and shape, the picture on the side, the brand of the mug or the place where you bought it. When you describe the quality of your product, the way it is made, its accuracy, the use of special materials, the millions of dollars you have invested in research and development, you are describing features. Benefits,

What's It Worth?

How much value is there in a glass of water?

If you are not thirsty and are not concerned about being thirsty in the future, if your teeth are clean, if you don't need cooling down, if your goldfish already has a home — then probably none.

But if you were thirsty would you buy a glass of water?

If the cost was 10 cents, probably yes.

If the price was $1, maybe.

If the water was going to set you back $100 then definitely no. Unless, of course, you are in the desert and have been without water for three days. Then, even at $1000, the glass of water is good value.

Value is relative.

Value is determined only by the customer.

Value is benefit minus cost.

on the other hand, are what those features can do for the buyer. Benefits cannot be determined by the maker or seller, only by the customer. This is why value is subjective. Furthermore, only some of a product's or service's features will be seen by the customer as benefits. As we have seen, those that are will vary from person to person, situation to situation and time to time.

Benefits Solve Problems

An understanding of benefits begins with understanding the psychology of the buying decision. All human behaviour is driven by our desire to satisfy needs. Sometimes, we cannot do this and then we have a problem. As you can see on page 27, it is this problem that sends us shopping. When we go shopping we look for solutions to our problems. Now you might sell products or services but your customers are buying solutions. If your customer sees at least one feature as providing a solution to their problem, they will conclude that the product or service is of benefit to them. For example, if you have a dull room and you go shopping and spot a brightly coloured cushion, you might buy it to brighten up your room. Your need was to feel cheerful. The problem is the room is dull so your need is not met. A feature of the cushion is its colour. You see that feature as solving your problem so it becomes a benefit. Note that you might be oblivious to its other features because your mind is focused on solving the particular problem you have at that moment.

Customers will see benefits only if the features of your product and service make sense to them. In other words, they must know how to use the solutions you provide. Much modern technology, for example VCRs, is undervalued because people do not understand how to make full use of it. As a result, they cannot extract the full benefits. The more complete the solution you provide and the more fully your customers are able to use that solution, the more benefits they will believe they have obtained. And the more value they will believe they have received.

Some companies, such as IBM, claim to understand this. Their marketing slogan is *Solutions for a small planet*. Similarly,

Benefits satisfy people's needs such as food, shelter, rest, comfort, safety, security, approval, personal growth, excitement, love, belonging, autonomy, respect, stimulation, social interaction, challenge, need to help others, support, attractiveness, prestige and entertainment.

Microsoft calls their service contractors *Microsoft Solution Providers*. Reflecting the need for more than customer service, they see these providers as being "in partnership with Microsoft to implement customer solutions". Many companies have discovered whole new business opportunities by switching their focus from selling products and services to solving their customers' problems. The photocopying industry is a good example, with companies such as Canon and Xerox developing new businesses by providing their customers not just with machines but with sophisticated document management services.

New Zealand Post certainly understands the importance of solving the customer's problem. A few years ago they sold stamps and collected government revenue and that was about all. Today, every post office is a full stationery shop set up for providing the total solution.

Many companies have discovered whole new business opportunities by switching their focus from selling products and services to solving their customers' problems.

One day I walked into the Post Office in Christchurch with a broken camera lens that I needed to ship quickly, cheaply and safely to Auckland — some 800 km away. I described my problem to the sales person behind the counter. She led me out into the store and showed me where I could get a pre-paid courier pack and then took me over to a shelf containing bubble packaging material. She left me while I took a pack of bubble packaging, opened it and wrapped the lens. Next, I went over to the pre-paid courier packs, selected the one that was the right size, put the lens inside and sealed it. Then I returned to the counter, paid for the goods, handed over my parcel and left the store knowing the lens would be in Auckland within 24 hours. Total solution. Great value. Compare that with my experience in Canada. I took an A4-sized envelope in to the post office and asked to send it from London to Woodstock, Ontario — a distance of 50 km. When I asked how long it would take to get there, the woman said it would take four business days. When I asked if there was a faster way, she said I could pay extra and send it Express Post but because it was not going from one main centre to another she could not guarantee it would get there any quicker! Where was the solution? Where was the benefit?

David McNaughton demonstrated the power of the complete solution when he founded the Public Affairs Resource

The Psychology of Buying

All people are driven by NEEDS

A need that is not met becomes
a PROBLEM

Your customer's problem is your reason for being in business.

People go shopping
for SOLUTIONS

Any feature of your product or service that solves
their problem will be perceived as a BENEFIT

**Any feature that does not solve the customer's problem
will be seen as waste.**

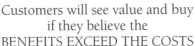

Anything customers must expend —
money, time and effort — will be seen
as a COST

Customers will see value and buy
if they believe the
BENEFITS EXCEED THE COSTS

27

Group, Canada's first fully integrated public relations firm. McNaughton saw the need for companies to have their total communications problems solved whether they involved communicating with government, the public, customers or staff. As a result, he blended together the functions of lobbying, public opinion polling and public relations. His experts poll, chart and interpret public opinion and then plan the most effective way to appeal to politicians and the media.

DuPont discovered how better solutions provide more benefits and result in a competitive advantage when they developed the Stainmaster carpet. Their market research identified a problem that customers had with all carpets — staining. They then set up a crash R&D programme to be the first with a solution. They worked closely with their customers — both carpet retailers and end-users. The result was the Stainmaster carpet, happier customers and a bigger market share.

By the same token, a bakery at the southern tip of New Zealand grew its export business by solving a problem for Japanese restaurants. The restaurants were having trouble making good-quality white sauce. Millar-Lange, one of the Goodman Fielder Milling & Baking sites, realised that they had a supply of good flour and milk and both the expertise and the equipment to manufacture the product. They presented Japanese customers with such a good and affordable solution to their problem that today Millar-Lange ships several tonnes of frozen white sauce to Japan every month. An unlikely product for a bakery, an excellent solution for their customers and a good business for the company.

One small business that understands the power of providing a complete solution is the Tutukaka Dive Shop in northern New Zealand. My friend lost his catch bag on day one of a two-day dive trip. When we returned to shore that evening we went to the dive shop to buy a new one, only to find they were out of stock. When the owner realized my friend's predicament he gave him his own bag to use the next day. "Here take mine. I'll sell you a new one the next time you're up here." My friend obtained a benefit and the retailer got a lot of goodwill, free advertising and customer loyalty.

To see how much benefit you are providing your customers, look at how well your products and services solve their problems. Look closely enough and you are likely to find opportunities to create even more benefits. Nearly all motel rooms in New Zealand, for example, provide tea and coffee making facilities in the room. Few North American rooms do. On the other hand, most North American motels have a 1 p.m. check out whereas in New Zealand it is 10 a.m. Motels in each country have an opportunity to provide a better solution, produce more benefits and gain a competitive advantage.

RULES OF BUSINESS
RULE 1. The customer is always right.
RULE 2. If the customer is ever wrong, read Rule 1.

Sign at Stew Leonard's Dairy in Connecticut. He has more sales per square foot than any other grocery store.

The Customer Is *Always* Right

If you are determined to be second to none, you must be convinced about two things. First, the customer is always right about the problem they have. Perhaps you do not understand their problem, but they still have it. Maybe it is not a problem for you, but it is for them. Perhaps you do not have the solution, but they still have the problem. Remember that no opportunity in business is ever lost. If you fumble the ball, your competitor will pick it up.

Secondly, you must be convinced that your customer's problem is your reason for being in business. If they did not have that problem, you would not have your business. Your job, then, is to solve your customer's problem. Perhaps you do not have the solution among your existing products and services. In that case, develop something new. If it works for the new customer, it might work for other customers. If so, you have just grown your business.

No opportunity in business is ever lost. If you fumble the ball, your competitor will pick it up.

But Often Wrong

It is not easy to identify your customers' problems because although your customers are always right about the problem they have, they are often wrong about the solution to their problem. Unfortunately, when customers come in they usually talk about the solution they want, not the problem they have. They might tell us, for example, that they would like a

Customers are always right about the problem they have. But they are often wrong about the solution to their problem.

2 mm drill bit, when in reality they want to hang a picture on a concrete wall. Most of us react to their request and if we have a drill bit in stock, we make a sale. There are two problems with this. First, if we do not have one in stock we send them away empty handed. They are disappointed and we have lost a sale. Secondly, even if we have one in stock, it might not be the best solution. Imagine that your customer goes home, drills the hole and hangs the picture. Later a neighbour comes in and tells them about a better way to hang pictures using a *whatsit*. What's more, he tells your customer that your store has *whatsits* in stock and you should have recommended them. You now have a dissatisfied customer and do not know it! They will probably not come back to you and complain, they will just tell everyone else about how you let them down.

Seek First To Understand

If your customer comes and asks for a solution, make sure you understand their problem before making a sale. Do not be like the computer store I dealt with recently. When I asked the price of their systems they asked me lots of detailed questions about the specifications of the hardware I wanted. They asked nothing about what I was going to do with the machine. Because it was important to me to have the computer up and running quickly, I paid extra to have someone come to my home and install it. When they came I was told that although the hardware was bundled with software for the Internet, getting the computer on-line and setting up e-mail had nothing to do with them. This, however, was my primary reason for buying the machine. The computer technician and I had a great deal of difficulty understanding each other. He

One Person's Box

In America, an air conditioner is little more than a box that keeps the room cool as cheaply and efficiently as possible. In China, it is a major consumer purchase and frequently a status symbol. Chinese customers will spend about as much time fussing over which make of air conditioner to buy as Americans would choosing a new car or an expensive hi-fi.

The Economist

was selling computer hardware (features). I was buying a communications solution (benefit).

It is a fool who tries to sell on the basis of a product's features because people buy only on the basis of benefits. The Lincoln was a car loaded with features. Within the luxury car market it was a technically superior car, even compared with the Cadillac. From the 1960s through to the 1980s, though, the Cadillac outsold the Lincoln by a margin of 6 to 1. Customers perceived value in the Cadillac that went beyond the product's features. Many Japanese automakers have fallen into this trap. Their traditional strengths have lain in their technical and manufacturing abilities, but one of the reasons for the decline in their market share over recent years has been their tendency to add costly features to their cars that customers simply do not want. Some subcompacts include side mirrors that vibrate to shake off the rain. Such a feature provides no benefit to many customers, but it does increase the vehicle's cost, thus diminishing the value of the car.

Think Benefits, Make Benefits, Talk Benefits

In fact, you can make a powerful sales presentation simply by asking questions that lead the customer to appreciate the benefits your product or service can offer them:

> *A benefit is a feature which the customer believes will solve their problem.*

- *"What is the biggest problem facing your company right now?"*

- *"Why is that a problem for you?"*

- *"How much is that problem costing you?"*

- *"What solutions have you tried already?"*

- *"How did they work out?"*

- *"Based on your experience, what do you believe would have to happen for that problem to disappear?"*

- *"If we could do that, how would it help you?"*

- *"What would it be worth to you to have that problem solved?"*

- *"So, if our company could train your staff better so they made fewer mistakes it would save you several hundreds of dollars each month?"*

- *"And if it cost only two thousand dollars to do the training then over twelve months you would be dollars ahead?"*

Simply by asking questions, you have led your customer on a journey where they visited their problem and reminded themselves of its cost. Then they saw a benefit and discovered its cost. By the journey's end, it was easy for your customer to calculate the value they would receive and make the decision to purchase.

Professional sales people first take the time to qualify their prospective purchasers. They ask questions and they listen. They try to understand which problems the customer is trying to solve and what is most important to that customer. Then, because they know their products inside out, they are able to sift through all their features and present those they believe will match the problem. If they are right, the customer hears the sales presentation and says to himself:

"Hey, that would solve my problem."

The next thing you know, the customer concludes:

"That product will benefit me."

Now all the customer has to do is calculate the costs of purchase and if the benefits outweigh the cost, they will perceive value and make the purchase.

The Costs Of Purchase

If value equals benefits minus cost, then another approach to gaining a competitive advantage is to reduce the costs your customer has to pay. Many business people believe that price is different from value, but this is a mistake. In the customer's eyes price is an important part of the value equation. Customer satisfaction depends on the answer to the question:

"Did I get sufficient benefit from this product or service to justify the price I paid?"

Usually, when we think of the cost of purchase we think only of the price, but price is just one of the costs people pay. As we shall see in Strategy 2 it is dangerous to compete on the basis of price alone. If you are aiming to win and not just survive, you must be aware of the other costs your customers pay and then work to reduce them (see Strategy 5). Apart from the purchase price, there is the *cost of ownership*. What are the installation or set-up costs of purchasing your product? What are the costs of on-going operation and maintenance? Customers take these into account when deciding whether to buy. Which would you consider to be better value: A cheap car that is expensive to run and requires a lot of maintenance or a more expensive car with low operating costs?

There are also non-financial costs. Every purchase takes *effort* — effort to research, effort to purchase, effort to install. In a world where we are all very busy, this can be a major cost. The easier you can make it for people to do business with you, the more value you will have created. One of the problems downtown retailers face is that shopping in the city centre takes too much effort. First you have to fight the traffic and then you have to find a place to park. The suburban malls are more convenient. Catalogue, telephone, TV or Internet shopping, grocery businesses who deliver to your home, airport valet parking, and low-maintenance homes are all examples of businesses that exist because people do not want to pay the price of effort.

Similarly, time is a cost. Who of us has too much time? Some businesses understand that the faster they can make things happen, the more value they add, but many do not. One Saturday afternoon my wife and I went looking for a bookcase for my study. I saw one I liked on display in a store for a couple of hundred dollars and went to the desk to buy one.

"Sorry," said the shop assistant. "We don't have any in stock. We'll have more in four or five weeks."

"Not interested," I said. "You've just discovered the basic law of retailing. You cannot sell what you don't have."

"Of course we can," snapped the assistant. "People just order it and wait."

A store across the road did better. They had a bookcase in stock which I liked, even though it was slightly more expensive. But they could not deliver it for two days. The store next

> *It is never a question of value or price because in the customer's eyes price is an important part of the value equation.*

> *Price is only one of the costs people pay to obtain a product or service. In the modern world, effort and time are big prices customers pay.*

Another big cost customers pay is the emotional cost — feelings of discomfort, anxiety and worry — that come from exposure to risk

to them understood the cost of time. Not only did they have a bookcase in stock (an even more expensive one, I might add), but when asked when they could deliver it the owner replied, "Can you be back home in 15 minutes?"

Another cost we pay when we buy something is *exposure to risk*. There are feelings of discomfort that are associated with purchasing or using a product or service. There is always anxiety in making a purchase. Have we made the right choice? Will the supplier perform as promised? Will we know how to use the new product? Will we get the expected benefits? Are there hidden costs of purchase or ownership? Will we see in the paper tomorrow that we could have got a better deal down the street?

You can compete on price alone but you probably will not win.

There are no free lunches. To gain your benefits, your customers have to pay a price. You can increase the value of your products and services by reducing these costs. Avoid the trap of competing on price alone, though. As we shall see in Strategy 2, it could destroy your business.

Summary

• **Creating value *is* your business.** The more you understand value, the more you will be able to understand your business.

• **The more you focus** all of your business activities and all of your people on creating value, the more successful you will be.

• **Value is both subjective and variable.** It can be defined only by the customer. It varies from person to person, situation to situation and from time to time.

• **Value = Benefits – Costs.** Your customers will conclude they are getting value when they consider that the benefits they derive from your products and services outweigh the costs they paid.

• **Benefits are not the same as features** because not all features will be seen as benefits — only those that solve the customer's problem.

• **There are many costs customers pay.** Price is only one. Others are the costs of ownership, and the effort, time and exposure to risk.

• **To increase the value you provide** increase the benefits you offer (see Strategy 6) or decrease the costs your customers pay (see Strategy 5).

• **Avoid falling into the price trap.** Price is only one cost and, as we will see in Strategy 2, it can be dangerous to compete on price alone.

How Are *You* Doing?

How well do the features of your products and services match your customers problems?

List your main products and services. Now list the features of each one. Then think of a key customer. Mark the features that they would consider to be benefits. Repeat this step for each of your major customers.

BENEFITS ANALYSIS

CUSTOMER:

Product or Service	Features	Benefits

How do you spend your time and other resources?

Do you spend time formally learning what your customers value? What have you learned in the last six months?

How would your staff define value?

How do you use that formula to improve your business?

Is your company focused on creating benefits or features?

Do you sell on benefits rather than features?

What are the main problems your customers are trying to solve?

What other problems do they have that you could solve?

What are the main costs your customers believe they pay?

What is the purpose of your business?

What would your staff say?

What is the unique buying proposition — the value — you
add to your customers that they cannot get elsewhere?

How are the changing demographics of our society affecting
your business?

What are the current consumer trends?

How are they going to affect your business?

✴ Strategy 2

Compete On Value, Not Price

In a competitive world it is tempting to compete on the basis of price alone. Because the Nineties is a time of economic constraint, price will always be an issue. But trying to be the lowest priced supplier is a dangerous strategy because it reduces your product or service to being just a commodity item. Moreover, justifying your price on the basis of your costs is a very difficult task. But perhaps the main reason why you should not compete on price alone is that it could destroy your industry.

The alternative is to compete by using a value-based strategy. Do things to make people feel good (give benefits) and remove the things that make them feel bad (reduce costs). There are several value-based strategies you can follow, ranging from giving people more benefits for higher costs, to fewer benefits for lower costs. In this competitive marketplace giving customers more benefits for less cost is the most powerful strategy. As benefits increase and costs decrease, the customer's perception of value soars.

Competing On Price Is Dangerous

In a dog eat dog market it is tempting to compete on the basis of price alone. Indeed, providing the same benefits as your competitors but at a lower price is the traditional way of trying to win business. It is also the worst strategy you can follow. If you compete on price alone you will probably not be second to none. You will be struggling to survive. Fight a price war and you relegate your product or service to being nothing more than a commodity item.

Price is only one component of value, and business leaders who ignore the larger picture of benefits and other costs will find themselves justifying their prices on the basis of their

What's the surest way to kill revenue, profit and customer loyalty? Get into a price war. Indeed, some of the biggest corporate losers today are those still fighting the old-fashioned price war.
Canadian Business
February, 1997

39

own cost structure. This is not a good position to be in because it is almost impossible to convince a customer that your costs are as low as they can possibly be. Anyway, your customers do not care what your costs are and they certainly do not see that it is their job to cover them.

Competing on price alone makes you vulnerable — especially if you have a hungry competitor with deep pockets who is prepared to take losses for a while just to get some business. And there are lots of them around in this marketplace! But understand this, if you do not compete on the larger issue of value, you will have no option but to compete on the basis of price alone.

It is a dangerous strategy to compete on price alone because unless you can truly be the lowest cost supplier, discounting your price means discounting your profit. Some companies have successfully used this strategy because of the low cost of their raw materials, the efficient way they produce their product or service, or because they have removed the intermediaries in their industry. The world's largest retailer, Wal-Mart, has reduced its operating costs by cutting out the middle man, effectively making retail stores out of warehouses. But even Wal-Mart does not try to have the lowest price on all items, just those where the public is price-sensitive. One of Wal-Mart's strengths is its ability to manage price variation. It is low cost where it has to be and it enjoys good margins in other areas.

The Canadian retailer Zellers made the mistake of getting into a price war with Wal-Mart by proudly proclaiming to the world that Zellers is the place "where the lowest price is the law". But because of Wal-Mart's ability to manage price variation so well, Zellers found itself in a war it could not win. Zellers also learned that falling profits from falling margins made a price war very costly. Bell Canada, on the other hand, avoided getting into a price war with its competitors. Recognising that when you are on top, you have the most to lose in a price war, Bell decided to win back customers by competing on value. It developed more benefits than its competitors and competed on service, reliability and support. This has been a successful strategy and Bell's market share has climbed back to over 70 per cent. Of course, their revenues remain intact.

But perhaps the biggest reason why you should not compete on price alone is that it could destroy your industry. Neither you nor your competitors will win in a price war, and long term, neither will your customers if some of you go out of business. A good example of this is the mobile telephone market. In the 1980s the market was owned by Motorola but then along came the Japanese and undercut their prices by 20 per cent. The Japanese promised the same quality for less money and customers took the bait hook, line and sinker. Motorola lost market share and, therefore, had no alternative but to fight back. The Japanese countered and prices plummeted. Eventually, Motorola "won" because they went lower than the Japanese were prepared to go. But what was the upshot of the price war? The profits were ripped out of the business, Motorola lost market share and customers learned that the only difference in value offered by the two suppliers was price. A high tech industry became a commodity business!

Some people who choose the strategy of being the lowest priced supplier are able to reduce their costs dramatically, but only by giving their customers fewer benefits in return. This can be a successful strategy if you are targeting a market that is attracted to a low-cost, no-frills supplier. Discount stores, self-service gas stations and kit-set furniture are all examples of this strategy. But remember, you can get away with reducing benefits only if your customers see the few benefits they do receive as being greater than the costs they pay. The problem is that they are often attracted to the offer but disappointed by their experience. The sweet taste of a bargain is often soured by the bitterness of poor performance.

The second thing you have to worry about with this strategy is that your competitors might match your price but also provide more benefits. This has been the discounter's main problem over the past few years. Being a low-cost, no-frills discounter in the grocery trade used to mean being low-price only. The time cost was high because the nearest store was further away than the neighbourhood supermarket and the aisles were not particularly well laid out. The effort was high because customers had to pack their own groceries and carry

We could have competed on price but frankly I don't think it's sustainable in the long-term.
Bruce Barr, Group Vice-President, Bell Canada

Unfortunately, all too many managers — and the experts who advise them — know more about winning pricing battles than about preventing those that are not worth fighting.
Thomas Nagel and Reed Holden, *The Strategy and Tactics of Pricing*

them out. The selection of food was not all that great either. Still, the low price gave the discounter a competitive advantage. Then others moved into that niche and started to match the price. To differentiate themselves further, the discounters had to reduce some of the other costs and increase the benefits they offered. In came more convenient locations and a better range of products — out went pack your own groceries and find-it-yourself shopping.

Meanwhile, "traditional" grocers have had to become more price competitive and have introduced no-frills house brands. The result is that the line between discounter and traditional grocer has become blurred. This has been the fate of most discounters in nearly all industries and so the fewer benefits

Mobil's Friendly Serve

Remember the self-service gas station where you happily pumped your own gas to save a couple of cents a litre?

Well, if you operate a low-cost, no-frills service station, watch out for Mobil. Attendants at some Mobil self-service stations are washing car windows, checking oil, putting air in tyres and sometimes even pumping gas, all for self-serve prices.

These services are part of Mobil's "Friendly Serve" which is being introduced throughout the USA. The programme was developed in response to customer survey results indicating customers wanted — surprise, surprise — fast and friendly service. According to Mobil's Midwest District Coordinator, Friendly Serve is designed to:

> *"Speed up the purchasing process and put a personality back into buying gas."*

Mobil hopes that Friendly Serve will help it to gain a competitive advantage through providing extra value. Says Jim Scheidegger, a Mobil station owner:

> *"Since almost everyone provides competitive service and the basics, this programme gives us a leg up on the competition. Most people appreciate the extra touch the service provides and will come back because of it."*

Scheidegger reports an increase in sales in his station since he implemented the Friendly Serve.

for low price strategy has, in reality, become one of same benefits for lower price.

If you are going to compete on the basis of price, then you had better be totally committed to that strategy. It is no good playing around with a small price reduction here and a few discounts there. You will simply get blown out of the water by someone who is serious about price reduction. Also, research shows that periodic discounting of price just encourages existing users of the product to stockpile. It does not persuade users of other brands to switch. The effect of these temporary price reductions is simply to deprive yourself of future sales.

There are more powerful value-based strategies to follow. Why play the same game as everyone else? Follow the example of Anita Roddick, founder of the Body Shop: "I look at where the cosmetics industry is headed and then go in the opposite direction."

There Is More To Buying Than Price

Fortunately, it is easy to compete on the basis of value because studies show nearly three-quarters of all customers buy for reasons other than price. The American Customer Satisfaction Survey done in 1995, for example, found that one telecommunications company, MCI, offered the best deal but got a lower customer satisfaction rating than Sprint, a rival supplier. What the public values most in telecommunications, the survey found, was a superior connection first, followed by brand recognition and good customer service. Then came price.

If you do not compete on the larger issue of value, you will have no option but to compete on the basis of price alone.

Most Australian shoppers choose their preferred retail outlets on factors other than price, according to the Australian Consumers' Association. A recent survey revealed that 75 per cent of consumers check the use-by dates and 70 per cent check the country of origin of the products before buying. Although Woolworths is not the cheapest supermarket chain in Australia, it had 34 per cent market share of groceries and its 1996 turnover was up nearly 10 per cent on 1995.

The Australian survey also indicated that shoppers attach a lot of importance to convenience and speed. Parking is important to them, as is not being kept waiting at the check-out.

The Australian research suggests that less than 20 per cent of customers are extremely price sensitive.

If price were the only thing that mattered we would all be driving Ladas!

Find Opportunities To Create Value

Your passion must be finding opportunities to create value. How can you give your customers increased benefits? Where can you reduce the costs they pay? How can you create situations where your customers would feel they would miss out on something if they did not purchase your product or service?

The essence of creating value is to make others feel good. People need hope, especially if the short-term outlook is gloomy. They need to think that things will be better in the future. This is particularly true today. Our parents experienced inflationary times. They knew that next year they would be earning more and that their house, which for most people was their nest egg, would have appreciated in value. Things are different now. We are reeling from the shocks of downsizing and high unemployment; many of us are still fearful of losing our jobs. Most of us are less well off in real terms than we were six years ago and, worse, the prospect for retirement is bleak. We know our government pension schemes will not be adequate to support us. We know we are not saving enough. The demographic trends tell us our houses will be worth less in the future. Indeed, an article in *Fortune* in mid 1996 told us that our parents were the first and last generation to be able to spend the last chapter of their lives in leisure and comfort.

Exploit all opportunities to create value. In a bleak world, give people hope. In a complex world, make things easier for your customers. Remove some of the anxiety from people's lives. Give them flexibility and mobility. Provide people with the information, the skills and the tools to take control of their lives. Be innovative, and produce new products and services that will give your customers the leading edge.

Look, Listen And Learn

The beginning of competing on value is to understand what motivates your customers to do business with you or your competitors. Discover what people currently value and what benefits they are seeking. One way to find out what people see as value-adding is to study advertisements. Admittedly, many advertisements reflect what the sellers and their advertising agencies see their products offering, but they are a good starting point. In one issue of *Fortune,* for example, there were 48 advertisements. Ten of these (21 per cent) stressed how *fast and convenient* their products and services were. Eight (17 per cent) appealed to the need for *comfort and luxury*. A further seven (15 per cent) described how their offerings would *make their customers successful*. Interestingly, thirteen (27 per cent) of these advertisements described either how good the company was because of its size, expertise or technology or how good the product or service itself was. These companies were advertising the features of their products and services, not the value they offer customers. They just do not get it, and that has got to be good news for anyone competing with them!

Another way to find out what people value is to watch what they do. Lowell Paxson and Roy Speer noticed three things. First, people like to shop. Secondly, people like to watch TV. Thirdly, they like to shop or watch TV whenever it suits them to do so. Paxson and Speer combined their observations into one commercially successful idea: The Home

Shopping Network Inc. It is an idea that produces hundreds of millions of dollars in revenue every year.

When Sharon Ludwig of Queensland, Australia was working in her husband's computer business, she found most of the people she was dealing with were men. To balance the equation she joined a number of women's networking groups and there she found that many women hated buying cars because of the bad experiences they had had. Out of that observation came a business idea: The Ladies Auto Search Service. The business finds the new or used vehicle that a particular client is searching for. Ludwig does not sell cars to people; she finds the cars that people want. Sales in the first year: $1,000,000.

If you understand how your customers view and interpret a given situation, you will understand what they value. One way to do this is to develop a relationship with them. A long-term relationship is best but even a short-term one will help. Intuit, the producers of personal and small business accounting software packages, stations staff at the check-out counters of some of the stores selling their products. When customers make a purchase, Intuit staff ask if they can visit them at home to watch how they use the software. This information is then used to drive improvements and new product development.

Opportunities to create value are all around you. You just have to learn to see them. We come across more opportunities in a single day than most of us could develop in a lifetime. It took thousands of years of walking on two legs before people had footwear that consisted of a left and a right shoe. Velcro was developed within the last forty years by someone pulling burrs off his trousers. For how many centuries have people done that without anyone seeing the opportunity for a product like Velcro? Opportunities to create value for your customers are in your hands right now. It is just a matter of closing your fingers around them.

You cannot assume you know what your customers value.

Do not assume you know what your customers value. Molly Maid, a Michigan (USA) company providing domestic help, surveyed 2300 customers and asked them what mattered most to them about a maid service. What did they value? Surprisingly, the most important factor was not cleaning. It ranked eighth on the list. At the top was safety and security. Molly Maid was able to use this information to refine their value strategy and gain a competitive advantage. Customers are full of surprises. Who would have thought that people would pay $2.70 for a litre of bottled water made especially for dogs? Or $23 for a two-ounce supply of *Le Pooch* perfume for dogs. Or $27 per hour to rent a dog in Tokyo. Value is in the eyes of the beholder! Get to know the beholders. Understanding what they value is your business.

A Non-Strategy For Competing On Value

Trying to compete by offering the same benefits as your competitors for the same cost is no strategy at all. Yet, some businesses are guilty of doing this. These are the businesses that have no strategic plan. The owners or managers believe they have a good product or service, they believe they are a good company to deal with, and they believe that if they explain these things to potential customers, sales will follow. Usually they do not. Professional businesses, like doctors, lawyers, accountants and dentists have been guilty of this for years. They seem to follow the philosophy:

> *I am a qualified person therefore people will come.*

Now that these business fields have become as competitive as everyone else's, this strategy does not work.

Xerox is just one example of a company that learned this lesson the hard way. They owned the technology, therefore they owned the market. When their patents expired, Xerox had competitors. But why worry? After all, they *were* Xerox. They nearly lost their business. Most North American consumer electronics companies did disappear. The U.K. automobile industry went the same way. Businesses following this non-strategy usually find the going so tough they end up using the *same benefits for less cost* strategy. The trouble is, the only cost they reduce is price, and as we have seen, that is a dangerous move. If you are having a hard time differentiating your product or service from that of your competitor, or if your market share is disappearing before your eyes, then you are probably following the *same benefits for same cost* strategy.

Value-Based Competitive Strategies

We should compete in business, then, on the basis of the benefits we provide versus the costs customers pay. Customers look at your products and services to see how these two variables relate to each other and then they compare them to those of your competitors. So should you. If you are serious about becoming second to none, your competitive strategy should be to increase the benefits you offer, decrease the costs your customers pay, or do both. As you can see on page 50, if the consumer perceives a high cost of purchase and little benefit, they will not buy. For them to change their minds you would have to increase the benefits or decrease the costs. If, on the other hand, they see that although the benefits are low and so are the costs, they are likely to buy. Be careful though, because as we have seen, they are also likely to become dissatisfied with their purchase afterwards.

More Benefits For More Cost

The customers tend to roll up into a big bundle the price, product attributes, perceived product quality...and to attach some value to that bundle. The bundle is then compared to competitive alternatives, and the "best value" is selected.

Dr Earl Naumann,
Creating Customer Value

Instead of going for the bottom end of the market with a *less benefit for less cost* strategy, you could try to gain a competitive advantage by providing more benefits at a higher cost. Historically, this strategy has worked well. Exclusive hotels, luxury car manufacturers and prestigious restaurants have succeeded in occupying a niche at the top end of the market, and without question there will always be a niche serving people who are prepared to pay more to get more. High-income people will pay to save time since the adage *time is money* is true for them. Hard-working people will often treat themselves to luxuries, and busy people will pay for convenience. Look for ways to "bundle" products and services. A gourmet restaurant might deliver a first-class meal along with a bottle of wine and a video. A theater might organize limousine transportation, pre-dinner drinks and a meal after the show. A travel agent might book meals at restaurants, trips to sights and obtain tickets for cultural and sporting activities.

Many companies, such as the Body Shop and Ben & Jerry's ice cream, are discovering that people will pay more if you are supporting a worthwhile social cause or following environmentally friendly practices. There is a cautionary note,

Value-Based Competitive Strategies

Same Benefits for the Same Cost
A non-strategy.

Same Benefits for Less Cost
Dangerous if the cost being reduced is price; good if other, non-financial costs are lessened.

Fewer Benefits for Less Cost
A viable strategy for the niche of discounter or no-frills. A crowded market these days.

More Benefits for More Cost
A viable strategy for the niche of "Exclusive or Top of the Line." Beware that even wealthy consumers are price sensitive.

More Benefits for the Same Cost
A powerful value strategy based on giving your customers something extra.

More Benefits for Less Cost
The most powerful value strategy and the one likely to be the most successful providing you focus on giving people something extra and on reducing all costs.

however. The fact that companies like Mercedes are moving into the smaller car market and airlines provide fewer first-class seats says something about the world we live in. Most people today are price sensitive — even the wealthy. We have all seen very well dressed customers shopping in the bargain basement!

More Benefits For The Same Cost

Many companies have discovered they can become number one by offering their customers more benefits for the same cost. McDonald's, for example, resisted the temptation to slash prices when faced with stiff competition, a slow economy and defecting customers. Instead, they developed *Extra Value Meals* which gave customers more product for the same money. Per store sales increased and profit margins started to look healthier as a result. Other fast-food chains have since followed suit.

[Note: More recently, McDonald's tried to slash prices and incurred the wrath of their franchisees.] Another example comes from grocery stores. Many are offering additional services such as cooking classes, coffee bars, dry cleaning, child care and in-store banking. At a Byerly's Fine Foods store in Illinois there are carpeted aisles, piano concerts and an in-store ice cream parlour. Yet another example is a garage that, when a car goes in for its regular servicing, does a free valet cleaning and touches up any paint chips. Or the car dealer who finds out what his customer's tastes in music are so that when they pick up their new car the owners find a couple of CDs in the glove box. There is a restaurant where the chef will write out the recipe if you liked the meal, and another serves free drinks and nibbles to people waiting in line for a table. A clothing store in Sydney, Australia provides large elegant changing rooms complete with music, potpourri and old books.

> *Successful more for the same strategies add things the customers perceive as being new and exciting benefits that are worth something in their eyes.*

Although many companies have been very successful using the *more benefits for the same costs* strategy, others have not fared so well. Why have some succeeded where others have

The Effects Of Cost Versus Benefit On Consumers

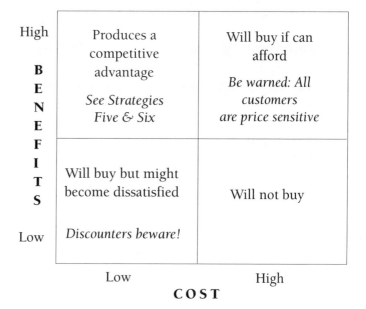

	Low	High
High BENEFITS	Produces a competitive advantage *See Strategies Five & Six*	Will buy if can afford *Be warned: All customers are price sensitive*
Low	Will buy but might become dissatisfied *Discounters beware!*	Will not buy

COST

failed? Firstly, this strategy is an old technique that, if not used properly, gets no reaction from the consumer. Getting 10 per cent more in your soft drink, a third more on the end of your chocolate bar or a free glass with every petrol fill-up does not excite many of us anymore. At one time these were benefits worth having, but not today. And that's the difference: Successful *more for the same* strategies add things the customers perceive as being new and exciting benefits that are worth something in their eyes.

More Benefits For Less Cost

The most powerful competitive value-based strategy is to give people more benefits for less cost, because as customers perceive benefits increasing and costs decreasing, their perception of value soars. For most businesses, the *more benefits for less cost* strategy must be the preferred approach because they find themselves in the middle of the pack with lots of competition.

Although you do not want to compete on the basis of price alone, for the foreseeable future price is always going to be a

Canadian consumers, since 1989, have been the most bargain-hunting, price-conscious types who won't part with their money unless they're getting incredible value.
Consultant Len Kubas

51

Three Steps To Using The "More Benefits For Less Cost" Strategy

1. Be at the low end of the price range.
   Nearly all of today's customers are price sensitive.

2. Reduce the non-financial costs customers pay (see Strategy 5).
   Often these costs are even less affordable to your customers.

3. Give them something extra (see Strategy 6).
   To have any impact the extra benefits you provide must be significant to your customer.

factor in the buying decision. Gone are the heady expansionist days of the 80s. According to Stephen Roach, chief economist for Morgan and Stanley: "The nineties are all about job constraints, income constraints and concerns about economic security." For the past seven to ten years, most people have found their real income has declined considerably. Recent surveys have shown a growing pattern of scepticism and frustration among people and, as a result, they are extremely price sensitive. It has been harder and harder to separate consumers from their money. It takes only the slightest hint of a recession to pressure people to postpone major purchases, as any modern retailer can tell you.

Not even strong brands are immune to this price sensitivity. IBM was able to regain its market share in Europe after losing huge chunks of business to various Asian clones but only after it got its price within 20 per cent of the competition. The IBM name was worth something but not at any cost. Similarly, Philip Morris had to take the drastic step of reducing the price of Marlboro cigarettes, sending shock waves through the stock market as a result. In spite of Philip Morris's investment in its brand, people were switching to cheaper products in alarming numbers. Said William Campbell, president of the company's tobacco unit, "Great brands are still great brands but you have to keep the price value in line with today's discerning consumers."

Using The "More Benefits For Less Cost" Strategy

There are three key steps to using this very powerful strategy. First, be at the low end of the price range. You do not have to be the lowest cost supplier but you must be within a range acceptable to your customer. Secondly, reduce the other costs involved in obtaining benefits from your products and services, such as cost of ownership, and the effort, time and exposure to risk. Often these are very expensive for your customers but can be reduced quite easily and at little cost to yourself (see Strategy 5). Thirdly, increase the benefits in your products and services without increasing the costs. Give your customers something extra (see Strategy 6) but remember, these extra benefits must be significant in your customer's eyes if they are to make an impact.

The next step then, is to learn to see the world through your customers' eyes.

Summary

• **Competing on price alone is a dangerous strategy** to use in a global economy. It can turn your product or service into a mere commodity item, destroy your profitability and potentially destroy your industry.

• **Providing outstanding customer value is the best way to differentiate yourself.** This means understanding the relationship between the benefits your products and services contain and the costs that are involved in getting those benefits — *as seen by your customer*.

• **There are a number of value-based strategies for competing and winning** ranging from the non-strategy of giving customers the same benefits for the same price as your competitor, to giving them more benefits for more cost.

• **The most powerful strategy** in this competitive market is to give your customers more benefits for less cost, including price.
  • Be at the low end of the price range.
  • Reduce the non-financial costs customers pay.
  • Give customers something extra.

• **The first step** to using a value-based strategy is to learn to look through your customer's eyes (see Strategy 3).

How Are *You* Doing?

Have you fallen into the price trap?

If so, what are the effects of this on your business?

What are the risks if you continue with this strategy?

If not, what are you competing on?
What makes you unique?

Do your products and services:

- Make people feel good?
- Give people hope?
- Uncomplicate their world?
- Make life easier?
- Lessen people's anxiety?
- Give people flexibility?
- Give people mobility?
- Give people control over their lives?
- Give people a leading edge?
- Help people to succeed?

Which value-based strategies are you using to compete to win?

- Same benefits for the same cost
- Same benefits for less cost
- Fewer benefits for less cost
- More benefits for more cost
- More benefits for the same cost
- More benefits for less cost

What are the risks in using your present strategy?

What would you have to be able to do to employ the "more benefits for less cost" strategy?

- To be at the lower end of the price range?
- To reduce the other costs your customers pay (see Strategy 5)?
- To give your customers something extra (see Strategy 6)?

How would your business benefit if you could do these things?

 **Strategy 3**

Look Through Your Customer's Eyes

Customers are not just important to your business, they are your business. Without them you have nothing. If you want to be second to none you must listen to your customers and learn from them, because, over time, your customers will tell you everything you need to know to run a successful business. As customers have had more choices, they have become more powerful. Today, they, not the producers, dictate what will be sold.

Looking after your customers through customer service is not a new idea. It has been popular for nearly 20 years. But good customer service is still rarely found because many business leaders look at the world from their own point of view, not their customers'. Even if it were happening, excellent customer service is not enough. The minimum aim must be to satisfy your customers. That at least requires us to understand our customers' needs and expectations, and to strive to meet them.

The Problem

Who Works For Whom?

Creating value involves getting something from your supplier and doing something to it so that it is worth more in your customer's eyes than it was before you laid your hands on it. The only person who can determine whether all your hard work and skill has produced value, of course, is your customer. Customers are not just important to your business, they *are* your business. If you do not agree, try living without any customers for 90 days. All of this means the only point of view worth worrying about is your customer's. You must learn to see the world through your customer's eyes not your own.

You must see your business from the outside in, not the inside out.

This all sounds like common sense but it is not a common occurrence. Most companies claim to be devoted to the satisfaction of their customers' needs but end up looking primarily after themselves.

Take the car rental company in Canada I dealt with recently. I had been renting a car from them on a monthly basis for several months. One day someone rang from the office and asked if I could bring the car in that day because the fleet manager had decided to sell it. The monthly lease was due to end the next week and so the car would have been returned then anyway. But no, that was not soon enough and I had to take an hour out of my day to travel across town to exchange the vehicle for another.

"I guess it seems crazy," said the branch manager, "to make you come in so we can take away your 1997 car and give you a 1996 model. But the fleet manager has decided to try to sell these."

"No, what is crazy is that you couldn't wait eight more days when it would have been returned anyway!"

Does your business work for the customer; or are you, through your policies, procedures and traditions, making the customer work for your business?

The fleet manager of this company needs to work out whether the business should work for the customer or whether the customer should work for the business. Ironically, but not surprisingly, the company's mission statement was total commitment to customer satisfaction; yet, here was a senior manager making a decision diametrically opposed to that goal. The branch manager and his staff, I might add, were very good. They not only understood my point of view but offered to make up for the inconvenience they had caused me. It seems the company was savvy enough to give each branch manager a slush fund he could use to make unhappy customers happy. Too bad senior management was not able to see their business through their customers' eyes and avoid these problems in the first place.

I once organized a meeting with my bank manager and suggested that it be held, for a change, in my office. When the time came for the meeting he was not there. After waiting a few minutes I decided to ring his office in case he had thought the meeting was to be held at the bank. But when I looked in the telephone directory there was only the name of the branch and a fax number — no phone number. There was, however, a message printed in bold:

For information about your account call 0800...

It is pretty clear what the bank is trying to do. If they can centralize account inquiries, they can minimize calls to the branches and make more efficient use of personnel. Nice for them, but when I called the 0800 number to find out where my manager was, no one knew. They solved their problem, but not mine!

One thing that really drives me crazy is the automated telephone answering system. You know, the sweet voice that gives you options:

If your aardvark is causing trouble, press 1
If your accordion is broken, press 2
If your acrobat is absent, press 3

Now, if you do not have an aardvark, accordion or an acrobat you are stuck. Sometimes, but not always, you can get in touch with a real live human being by pressing 0. Then again, if you do you are just as likely to hear:

Sorry, there is no one here to take your call.

Click.

If you are fortunate enough to be given a relevant option, after you make a choice you are likely to hear:

If you are inquiring about your account, press 1
If you wish to order, press 2
If you have a complaint, press 28561285799386

Having got this far, you hear a phone ringing and then a voice says:

Unfortunately, all of our agents are busy at the moment. Your call is important to us, please stay on the line and someone will be with you one day.

Too bad your call is not so important that they would have enough people answering the phone to avoid you having to spend the next 30 minutes listening to canned music. Eventually, usually after 28 refrains of Greensleeves, you hear:

If you wish to continue to hold, press 1
If you can't remember why you've called, press 2
If you can't remember who you are, press 3

I am sure this system makes it easy for the company to handle calls, but it does not make it easy for the caller. Why would companies pay so much money for an 0800 number and the technology to encourage people to call and then have so few people available that when customers do call they are looking at frustration and delays? The resulting stress level is so high that all 0800 numbers should carry the disclaimer:

Warning: Using this service can consume valuable periods of your life and could be hazardous to your mental health.

More and more research is indicating that customers hate these phone systems with a passion. The backlash cannot be far away.

Still, you are lucky if the people you want to talk to can be contacted at all. A friend of mine in Canada was having some trouble with a new gas stove she had purchased. She did eventually manage to reach a real person, but when she asked to speak to the customer services manager she was told he did not have a telephone! (I don't make these up, honestly.)

Looking From The Inside Out Is Dangerous

Treat your customers as if you had to live with them in a very small room for the rest of your life.

The more you understand about how your customers look at the world, the more you will understand about your business. Knowing all the technical details about your products and services is not enough these days. You must know what people do with them. I once ran a seminar for senior managers and directors of an electricity company. It became clear to them that they knew almost everything that needed to be known about generating and distributing electricity but next to nothing about how their customers used it. Although they were initially taken aback to discover how little they knew about their customers, overall it did not seem to bother them. Interestingly enough, that company does not exist any more. It has been taken over by a neighbouring power board who did understand more about the people who ultimately paid their wages.

When you assume that you know what your customers want you can pay a big price. Ford built the Edsel because it looked like a good idea to them. Customers didn't agree. Coca Cola thought the customer would like New Coke. They didn't. An ice cream manufacturer in New Zealand thought a new product launched by their competitor would never catch on. They were wrong. It captured 33 per cent of the novelty ice cream market within three months of being released. All of these companies thought they knew best what their customers wanted.

All of these companies thought they knew best what their customers wanted.

One example of looking at the world from the inside out is the presentation I heard not so long ago from some senior managers of a steel manufacturer. The first point they made was that their company had recently transformed itself from a state-owned monopoly into a customer-focused business. They then went on to describe a new product they were developing for the agricultural market. They had formed a joint venture with the inventor of this equipment because they saw it as a way of using more steel. If the product caught on, they told us gleefully, steel consumption in their market would increase appreciably. Not once during their presentation was there any mention of market research or data about customer needs. One of the audience noticed this and asked the steel company managers how sales were going. "Not too good. We've only sold seven so far although we've manufactured thirty-five. The market here seems to be small but we are optimistic it will grow."

I guess sales will increase once farmers realize that by buying the product they can help the company sell more steel!

For years, Proctor and Gamble dominated the toothpaste business in the United States. Through the 1980s they had a 40 per cent share of the market. Over the years, P & G assumed that customers were more concerned about health and hygiene than looking good, so they focused on developing products that addressed therapeutic needs and ignored cosmetic ones. Then small, start-up companies saw a gap in the

Clearly a key to successful selling is this: Find out how your customers want to buy and sell it to them that way.
James Champy,
Re-engineering the Corporation

61

market. They identified a need that P & G had missed and developed a toothpaste with a baking soda base. This sub-category now accounts for 30 per cent of the market and one of the early players, Methadent, is now the number three toothpaste in America with 11 per cent market share.

If you worry more about yourself than your customers you will lose business. Once a friend of mine was ringing some car rental places in Toronto when one businessman he had just called interrupted him and said quite curtly: "Call me back on this number."

"Why would I want to do that?" my friend asked. "I'm talking to you now."

"But this is my cellphone."

In North America, the receiver of the cellphone call pays the bill, not the caller, so I can understand that he wanted to reduce his costs. But he could have at least offered to call his customer back instead of expecting the customer to make a second call to him. Needless to say, my friend never did ring back and the salesman lost nearly $2,000 worth of business. Still, he did save a dollar on the phone call!

I saw more business being lost when I was having breakfast on a patio at a restaurant in Canada one sunny summer's morning. A party of four walked up and asked the waiter for a table. When he showed them one outside, the woman asked to sit inside.

"Sorry, we only serve breakfast outside."

"But I have hay fever and it is very uncomfortable for me to sit out here. Do you not have a table inside?"

Since I was sitting by a window I looked inside and saw a restaurant full of empty tables all set up and ready to be used. I expected the waiter to solve his customer's problem, but instead I heard him say: "We only serve breakfast outside. You could try the restaurant down the street."

Thirty dollars worth of business walked away. Now, this was not really the waiter's fault. His customer relations, his attitude towards his job and the service he provided were otherwise good. The trouble was the company policy and its culture of putting the business first.

Many Are Reluctant

Although it is dangerous to see the world from inside the company out, many companies appear to be reluctant to see themselves as their customers see them. Sure, they do customer satisfaction surveys, but mostly they want numbers, not qualitative information. When they do get customer feedback through complaints, many become defensive and make excuses instead of notes.

> *Torture the data until it confesses.*

Even when they get the numbers, many do not take heed. Twenty-five years ago, J.D. Power approached the Big Three US automakers and suggested he could help them to learn more about their customers and what they thought about the cars the Big Three made. Power had worked for both Ford and GM doing customers surveys, but back then, according to Power, the automakers wanted research that would confirm what management believed was right for their customers: "When we were doing research for them, we used to have a saying 'Torture the data until it confesses.' They weren't really interested in finding out what the customers were thinking."

When Power first approached the Big Three about doing unbiased independent surveys, he got the cold shoulder.

Market Bloopers

Companies who failed to understand their customers' world.

- The Ronald McDonald white-face promotion failed in Japan. White face means death.

- Coca Cola had to withdraw the 2-litre bottle in Spain. Few Spaniards have refrigerators big enough.

- The Chevy Nova bombed in Spain. In Spanish "no va" means "does not go".

- General Foods squandered millions trying to introduce cake mixes into Japan. Only 3 per cent of homes had ovens.

- Phillips shavers and coffee-makers had a slow start in Japan. The shavers were too big for small Japanese hands, the coffee-makers too big for small Japanese kitchens.

- Crest toothpaste failed in Mexico. No one cared about preventing tooth decay and they did not like scientifically based advertisements.

- Hallmark Cards bombed in France. The French dislike syrupy sentiment and usually write their own cards.

Undeterred, he borrowed money and conducted his own research into customer satisfaction and vehicle quality. He then tried to sell the results to the automakers. Again, he ran into a brick wall. But the Japanese automakers were interested. They wanted to get ahead of the Americans so they bought and studied Power's survey results. It paid off.

By the mid-1980s, the Big Three were forced to listen to Power's data, too. Some say that Power has been instrumental in the American auto industry's comeback. Now, the European car industry is in trouble. Recently, Power visited some of the leaders of Italy's automobile manufacturers. He offered to help them to understand how their customers saw them and their cars.

Guess what reaction he got.

What Do Your Customers See?

Is your business providing good customer service? Have you asked your front-line staff? Your customers?

It has long been believed that customer service is the cornerstone of commercial success. Customer service is important, of course, but there are two problems with this concept. First, most managers believe their business is doing a good job of providing customer service. If you are one of these, I have two questions for you. Have you asked your front-line staff what they think? Have you asked your customers?

The second problem is that to focus on customer service can be dangerous. When most companies think about customer service they think about what they do for the customer. But what you do does not really matter. What matters is what your customers need and what they think about what you do. Your performance is your customers' reality but your reality is *their* perception of your performance. The airline industry, for example, has conducted research and found that what matters most to air travellers is on-time performance. Consequently, all airlines measure departure and arrival times quite closely. The problem is that nearly all companies define on-time as being plus or minus 15 minutes of the scheduled time.

"But," says Canadian Airlines CEO, Kevin Jenkins, "plus or minus fifteen minutes is not on time to most customers." From an airline's point of view, they may be performing well. but from the customer's point of view, their performance is poor.

What do your customers see when they look at how you present your products or services to them? Alpha-Beta Foods, one of the first self-service grocery stores, learned the hard way that their view of their store and their customers' view were quite different. Alpha-Beta Foods stocked their shelves by placing products in alphabetical order, believing it would make shopping easier for their customers. When business dropped off they started asking questions and found that their customers were not thrilled with the asparagus being next to the ant poison!

> *For your customers, your performance is their reality. But your customers' perceptions of your performance is your reality.*

How Customer Friendly Is Your Business?

I recently visited a bird sanctuary on Australia's Gold Coast. From the moment my family, my retired parents and I arrived it became clear that the Rule Book was king. When we paid to enter, the clerk at the entrance refused to give my 80-year-old mother the senior citizen's discount because she did not have identification with her proving she was over 60. "I can see she is over 60," said the woman, "but our policy states she must be able to show proof of age."

The day continued like that. Attendants refused to open gates to let my parents take short-cuts, making them walk a couple of hundred metres further than was necessary. We were told to get off a little train (the rides were free) at the end of the line and walk to another station so we could get back on the same train. The rules said you could not stay on while the train moved from the last station to the first, and everyone had to begin at the start even though it was a circular route. I got the feeling that the animals and birds in the park were very well looked after. Too bad the customers were not.

In August of 1986, Lee Iococca gave a speech at the annual Chrysler Dealers convention. He set out to tell his dealers how they could grow their businesses in the coming year. Iococca's message was brief and to the point: "To succeed, all you have to do is to memorize four words. Here they are: 'Make someone like you.'"

All car dealerships are alike. Shop around and you will find the same types of cars, colours and range of options. The same will be true of your business. And why should anyone do business with you instead of your competitor? Give them a reason: Make them like you.

Most business people — and professional people are very guilty of this — have no idea how unfriendly, bureaucratic and overwhelming their businesses appear to their customers when they first walk in. Tomorrow morning, when you walk into your place of business try to see it through the eyes of someone who has never been there before and who may be feeling nervous, stressed or in a hurry. Is it easy for people to find you? It is clear to them where they must go for help or what they must do to get their problem solved? Are expensive furnishings intimidating to people not accustomed to such surroundings?

Is your store so cluttered that people do not know where to start to look for things? Recently, I went into one of the mega-book stores that are springing up throughout North America. At the business section, I was confronted with hundreds of books sitting on shelves with only their spines showing, just as they would be on your bookshelf. I stopped looking after five minutes. How long can you concentrate with your head at right angles to your body?

How Friendly Are Your Signs?

What do your customers see when they look at your signs? Are they friendly, inviting and customer-orientated? Or, are they really saying; *"We look after ourselves first."* Does your business spend hundreds of dollars on advertising and then greet all customers with such cheerful greetings as:

> *Management reserves the right to refuse service to people who are improperly attired.*
>
> *All sales are final.*
>
> *No cheques cashed without prior approval.*
>
> *If not consuming food, please vacate the table.*
>
> *This is not a waiting area.*
>
> *No loitering. Time limit 20 minutes.*
>
> *Customers' bags will be opened for inspection.*

And Your Staff?

What about when your customers look at your staff? Some companies get the signs right and then their staff blow it. Like the bank I went into which had a wonderful sign:

> *Excellent customer service is our daily goal.*

The trouble was that the tellers serving people never smiled, made little eye contact and virtually no conversation. Now which do customers believe — a sign or their personal experience?

Are your staff friendly? I once shopped in a state-owned liquor store in Ontario, Canada and when it came to paying for my purchases, the first and only words the cashier uttered were when he gave me back my change. He said, "Have a nice day." I am sure he meant it.

Are your staff happy? Once, while flying with one of New Zealand's two main domestic airlines, the passenger services agent was so miserable and curt that I asked her if she liked living in her house and eating three meals a day. Obviously surprised at my question, she stammered that she did. "Well, then, you'd better start enjoying serving me because we customers," I said pointing to everyone standing in line, "are paying for those things. All we have to do is walk fifty paces to the competition's counter to find someone who is happy to help us."

She had a bit of an attitude adjustment after that.

Are your staff helpful? I once saw a man laden with baggage rushing to catch a plane at Toronto Airport. He had got through security and was, with arms full of luggage, trying to find the gate. As he struggled past an airline employee who was standing at her counter with nothing to do, he cried out: "Excuse me, which gate for Atlanta?"

Quick as a flash and without even glancing at her computer terminal she replied: "I don't know, sir. You'll have to check your boarding pass."

Are your staff competent? Are your customers encountering people who have the product knowledge and understanding of how your business works, so that they are able to deliver what customers want? I once ate in a seafood restaurant in Queensland, Australia where you select the wine you would like from a large refrigerator with glass doors. Their selection was excellent. In fact, it was so good, I was having trouble making a decision. When the Maitre 'D who had been at that restaurant for 12 years walked past I asked him if he could recommend a good white wine. "No," he said, "I don't drink

Pay Your Staff To Be Customers

A restaurant in Florida, Chef Allen's, pays its staff to eat at a competitor's and then report their findings.

Owner Allen Susser pays his staff US$50 to dine at other restaurants with a similar cuisine to his own. They then return to work and present a short oral and written report to the rest of the staff. Each of the company's 30 employees visits a competitor's restaurant every three months.

According to Susser, the benefits have far outweighed the costs of operating the programme. One cook, for example, sampled excellent food served on a cold plate. He was fussier about warming the plate after that.

There are other benefits, too. Employee turnover is low at Chef Allen's and the restaurant is regularly booked out. It also gets very good reviews in the press.

Allen Susser has learned that paying employees to be customers can be good for your business.

wine." I guess he misunderstood my question. I was not asking about his habits with regards to the taking of libation but whether, in effect, he knew his job.

Are your staff pleased to have customers? Do they show it? Tell your staff to smile, even on the telephone. It comes across in their voice. Get them to look at their customers and to engage them in pleasant conversation. Encourage them to make people smile. Everything you do should be personal. Use the word "I" and avoid the word "policy". Your customer's experience with your business should be a pleasant one.

And Your Policies?

Would your customers say that your policies and procedures appear to be designed with them in mind? One Friday night I was in a wine store at about 6 p.m. salivating over the selection when a delivery truck pulled up. The driver jumped out and started wheeling in box after box of liquor.

"Don't bring that stuff in here at this time of night," said the owner. "I have nowhere to store it and I have no time right now to price it and put it on the shelves. This is the time when I'm busiest serving customers. I ordered the stuff three weeks ago, why must you deliver it at this time of night?"

"OK, OK," said the driver. "What's the latest time I can deliver the goods in the afternoon?"

"Four o'clock," said the store owner.

"Not possible," said the driver.

"OK, five o'clock," countered the store owner.

"No way," replied the driver.

"Well, leave it on the truck until the next day," suggested the owner.

"No can do," said the driver. "Company policy says if it's on the truck it must be delivered that day."

And with that he walked out, got in his truck and drove off into the sunset leaving another dissatisfied customer in the dust.

Even charitable organizations who are literally begging for money fall into the trap of having policies that work better for them than for their donors. One day a man telephoned our house collecting money for a helicopter rescue service.

"We're desperate for money because the government is cutting our funding," he pleaded.

"OK," said my wife. "We'll give ten dollars."

You must see your business from the outside in, not the inside out.

"We cannot accept donations that small," said the caller. "If it's anything less than twenty dollars, it's not worth our while coming to collect the money."

"Well, that's a shame," said my wife. "I'm happy to give you ten dollars but I don't feel like giving any more than that."

"I understand," said our intrepid fund raiser. "I've had quite a number of people tell me that."

Emergency services can sometimes make the same mistake. I once read about a fire department that insisted citizens

Be A Happy B.E.E.

I came up with an awareness tool to remind everyone in the restaurant to focus on friendly service. Instead of referring to them as crew members, I called them "Happy B.E.E.s." "B.E.E." stood for B — bad moods stay at home; E — eye contact with the customer; E — every day.

Naturally there were skeptics, and some of the teenagers thought the whole idea was corny at first. But soon they realised it was much nicer serving customers who smiled back. The key that made the programme work was being a Happy B.E.E. myself. We reinforced the practice with T-shirts, caps, buttons, and even Happy B.E.E. bucks, redeemable for gifts. I also informed the team of our sales trends, which increased.

The task was to inspire an entire group to exceptional service. The Happy B.E.E. technique helped them smile, which made the customers happier — and made work more fun. And, instead of expecting new sales to fall from the sky, we gave our customers a compelling reason to come back.

Three months after I became manager — two months into the Happy B.E.E. programme — our sales were more than 20 per cent over projection. My district manager revised the projection to $1 million for the year and implemented the Happy B.E.E. programme in all seven stores in his district. Soon they were showing the greatest ever year over year comparable sales increases in the larger region.

Leadership is Common Sense Herman Cain,
CEO, Godfather's Pizza Inc.

phone their central emergency number to report fires instead of calling the local fire station direct. One day they came to work to find a message on their answerphone saying a house was on fire. When staff arrived at the scene they found the fire had been burning for 12 hours.

What do your customers see when they attempt to return some defective merchandise? Do they get an apology and a replacement or do they get interrogated and then told that either nothing can be done, or worse, nothing will be done unless proof of purchase is provided? I once tried to return something inexpensive — a $16 desk lamp that I had purchased a couple of weeks earlier. The lamp had failed and I needed it replaced. The first thing the shop assistant did was ask for proof of purchase. I told him that I do not keep receipts for items that small and that I would not expect such a simple piece of equipment to fail.

The response was to refuse to do anything without the sales slip. Customers do not argue in such situations. They leave. They take their business elsewhere. And they tell others how terrible the service is at that store.

What happens in your business when customers are unhappy and come to complain? Do staff get defensive? Do they make such unhelpful comments as:

"Gee, no one else has ever complained about that."

Do they explain why it was not their fault but someone else's?

- *"That problem is caused by our supplier. They should never have sent the product out like that."*

- *"We can't do what you want. That other sales person should never have agreed to do it."*

- *"We've never done business that way. I can't understand why anyone would have promised that."*

Such calming and soothing words for the customer to hear!

The response that really drives me crazy is when you have a problem with a certain department and wish to make a complaint:

"Do you have a customer complaint system?"

"Yes, sir. Why?"

"I would like you to record a complaint for me. I am not happy waiting three weeks for a battery for my $10,000 laptop."

"If you want to make a complaint, sir, you have to contact Customer Services. I'll give you the number."

"Thank you, but I don't want the number. I've spent enough time on this already. Just record my complaint, please."

"But Customers Services handles complaints, sir."

"Then you contact them for me, please."

"I can't do that, sir. I'll give you their number."

"Aaaaaaaaaaaaaaggggghhhhh!"

Get Inside Your Customer's Skin

Business is like tennis. Those who serve poorly, lose.

All of these are specific examples of a generic problem. Despite the hype, we usually fail to see our business from the customer's point of view. Learn to get inside your customer's skin and walk around in it for a while. See what they see. Find out what they think about and understand their point of view. Focus on what is most important to them, not you.

As Howard Russell, a New Zealand-based marketing consultant, has pointed out, for years we have concentrated on selling, which is the activity we engage in, instead of buying, which is the activity the customer is interested in. So we focus on our *unique selling proposition* instead of the customer's *unique buying proposition*. Says Russell: "Customers are interested in buying, not selling."

Retailers who think about selling offer customers lots of choices. Incredible Universe, for example, offers Canadian shoppers 335 models of televisions to choose from. But customers do not want that many choices. They want to buy and buying involves making decisions. What customers need are retailers to simplify the decisions for them. Wal-Mart understands this and offers its customers two choices — the market leader and the second market leader. Incredible Universe is struggling and Wal-Mart is the world's largest retailer. The price of failing to see the world from the customer's perspective is very high!

I do not suppose seeing the world from the inside out is a problem in your business but here is a way you can check just in case. If you ever find yourself saying:

- *"Sorry, we cannot do that because…"*
- *"Our policy states…"*
- *"We have do it that way because…"*
- *"Our procedures require that…"*
- *"No one has asked for that before."*
- *"It cannot be done that way."*
- *"It has to happen this way because…"*

then you are guilty of committing this cardinal sin.

The Solution

Get The Culture Right

Your customer must come first, last and always. This belief must be held not just by management but by each employee. Is everyone in your business passionate about finding ways to create value for your customer? If you asked each employee these three questions, how would they answer?

1. Who do you work for?

2. Who is your boss?

3. Who pays your wages?

Getting everyone to put the customer first is a leadership issue. In other words, it is up to you. Your staff must see that you believe in the philosophy:

If you, the customer, wins; then we win.

You must speak about it constantly. You must make policies and decisions consistent with this philosophy, and, of course, you must practice what you preach. If you talk "customer first" but act "profits first" you know which your staff will think you believe in most.

Having mission and vision statements that put the customer first and which stress the customer's primary position in the commercial transaction are important leadership tools.

Most companies, however, have very weak and self-serving vision and mission statements. Note these examples:

- *We will be number one in our industry.*

- *Customers will choose us first.*

- *We will become the preferred supplier of widgets.*

- *We will have the largest market share.*

How nice for these companies who clearly are putting themselves first and seeing the world from the inside out! Because business is the enterprise of creating value, your vision statement should talk about how you will create value for your customers. For example, a grocery store might say:

- *We aim to make your family healthy.*

An insurance company:

- *We provide peace of mind.*

Or a furniture store:

- *We will transform your house into a home.*

You can convince everyone of the importance of the customer only if they see that all policies, procedures and decisions put the customer first. Review your existing policies and procedures to make sure they do. Also, do regular audits of major management decisions (like the one made by the fleet manager of the car rental company I described at the beginning of this section) to make sure they are consistent with your "customer first" philosophy. It is a good idea to involve some of your staff in these reviews — particularly front-line staff who have constant customer contact.

If your culture is right, everyone will understand that customers want solutions, not problems. Everyone will work to help customers find a solution even if they cannot provide it themselves. Never send a customer away empty-handed. Never say no. Give them something, even if it is only the name of another place to try. One reason why customer service is so poor from the customer's point of view is that customers walk away without their problem being solved. If you ever hear yourself or your staff saying:

- *"Sorry, we don't carry that item."*

- *"We don't do that work."*

- *"Sorry, we are out of stock."*

- *"It isn't working right now."*

- *"Sorry, our office is closed."*

- *"It can't be done."*

- *"Sorry, our technicians are all out right now."*

- *"Yeah, that happened to me one time."*

- *"No one else has ever had that problem."*

- *"Gee, I don't know."*

then you know you have missed the boat.

Customers do not want to hear the word "no". They are looking for solutions, not problems. One company in New Zealand — Westco Lagan, who are manufacturers of specialist timber products — understands this. On every employee's desk and on the walls throughout the workplace are signs that read: *"Never say no."* You may not always have the solutions your customer is seeking, but there is always something that you *can* do. What customers want to hear is:

We don't sell products. We capture customers.
Alfred Zeien,
CEO, Gillette

- *"I cannot do what you ask, but what I can do is …."*

- *"We don't have what you want but I'll tell you who does."*

Transform Employees Into Business People

You cannot survive in this business environment if you and one or two other senior people think like business people but everybody else acts like employees. Employees think about their jobs. Business people think about their customers.

Your staff should treat their customers as if their future depended upon them — because it does. It would be easier for your staff to appreciate this if they knew the value to your business of each customer. Many business leaders do not know this information themselves and those that do rarely think to share it with their staff. But it makes a big impact if you do.

Employees think about their jobs. Business people think about their customers.

75

Holmes Packaging, one of the most exciting and successful packaging companies in Australasia, have discovered this. Their commitment to both their customers and their staff is outstanding. Every year for five years they have closed the business and taken all staff away for a two-day live-in retreat to discuss business issues, share the company's future plans and do staff training. One year they arranged for a member of their sales team to make a presentation about the customers in his territory. With a map on the wall, he took everybody on a tour of the South Island of New Zealand. He would point to a town, tell them which customers were located there, what kind of business they operated, which products they bought, in what quantities and what the value of the orders were. It was a very entertaining and informative presentation. But what was fascinating was to hear people's reactions afterwards. I heard one woman say: "Gee, I never knew an order from the Acme Potato Company was worth that much money. I always thought of them as being a real nuisance because those bags are hard to make. Now I see they pay my wages."

Do your staff know what your customers are worth? This is a vital statistic which might help them to react more positively when that customer becomes demanding. If you ran a grocery store, you could expect the lifetime value of a customer who spends $150 each week for twenty years to be $156,000. A garage could expect a customer gassing up once a week to be worth between $30,000 and $40,000. Someone who got their hair cut every two weeks would have a lifetime value of over $10,000 and a customer spending $5,000 a year with an insurance company would be worth $100,000. They are impressive figures because they tell how much you have to lose if your customers do not come back. If many defect, and you cannot find replacements, you are dead. There is nothing like the fear of death to focus the mind!

Your staff should treat their customers as if their future depended upon them — because it does.

Turning employees into business people is hard, but you will be more successful if you try to change people's behaviour rather than their attitudes. Establish a process requiring staff to sit down with their customers — be they internal or external customers — to identify their needs and requirements. Next, your staff should turn what their customers have told them into performance specifications which then become the targets they aim to achieve. Finally, your staff should measure their performance against these standards. This is an on-going process, of course, with staff meeting with their key customers every two or three months. All of this works best if people are working in teams.

> *The best way to change people's attitude is to change their behaviour. Set up procedures and processes that require staff to do things differently.*

Seek Answers From Your Customers

I firmly believe that if you listen hard enough your customers will tell you everything you need to know to run a successful business. Levi Strauss learned this early in his career and it helped him to build the clothing empire that bears his name today. In 1853, Strauss's customers, gold miners in California, told him that the pockets on his jeans were not strong enough.

Five Steps To Getting To Know Your Customers

Everyone in your business needs to think like business people. Employees think about their jobs; business people about their customers. Organize your people into natural work teams.Focus them on their customers by asking them to go through the following five steps:

1. Identify their outputs

Each team should list all of the products and services that it produces and passes on to people in other teams.

2. Identify their customers

Anyone outside the company or any team within the company who uses an output is that team's customer.

3. Discover their customers' needs and requirements

The team should meet with or survey each of their customers to find out what they require. The team should begin with its most important customers first. Face to face meetings are best. Asking the right questions is critical. (See page 82)

4. Set specifications

The most important of the customer's requirements should be turned into specifications. A specification is always measurable, e.g, answer the phone within two rings.

5. Measure your performance

The team should constantly measure its performance to ensure they are meeting the specifications they set for themselves.

Their tools and ore samples were easily ripping the fabric. Strauss listened and with the help of Jacob Davis, a tailor in Nevada who was hearing the same things from his customers, devised a solution. The answer was to use rivets to reinforce the pockets. The idea was simple and effective. Better yet, it boosted sales. In the first year, Strauss sold 21,600 riveted pants and coats to miners, lumberjacks, cowboys and farmers throughout the West.

The Ford Motor Company's success in developing the 1994 version of the Mustang is another great example of what can happen when you listen to your customers. Ford invited 200 loyal customers, who included members of Mustang Clubs, to become involved in the design process. They reviewed and critiqued the prototypes and also drove Ford's competitors' products such as the Camero and the Firebird. In essence, these loyal customers helped Ford to understand what made a Mustang a Mustang in the eyes of the consumer. For example, when designers suggested the 94 Mustang have a four-cylinder engine and front wheel drive, the 200 hundred "advisers" collected 30,000 letters from fellow club members and Mustang owners saying that Ford could make a four-cylinder front wheel drive sports car if they wanted to but they had better not call it a Mustang. As far as the consumer was concerned, a Mustang is an eight-cylinder rear wheel drive vehicle. With the help of its customers, Ford brought the new model to market in 25 per cent less time at 30 per cent less cost than usual. Moreover, the entire year's production was sold out within a few months of the model being released.

KFC (Australia), thanks to its marketing director, Peter Waller, was able to grow its business by watching its customers. Waller noticed that families frequently ordered four of KFC's value meals, so he linked the four into one mega-meal that would offer enough food and variety to suit a whole family. It was hugely popular.

Even small, struggling businesses can benefit from reaching out and hearing their customers. Katherine Barchetti of Barchetti Shops in Pittsburgh was losing customers. To find out why she sent out three thousand letters asking people why they had stopped coming to her stores. Two hundred

Six Steps To Looking Through Your Customers' Eyes

1. Transform employees into business people.

2. Seek the answers from your customers.

3. Focus on customer satisfaction.

4. Measure customer satisfaction.

5. Bring the customer into the workplace.

6. Capture what you learn.

and ninety replied and over the next few months she wrote back to each one, fired unfriendly managers and modified her pricing policy. Based on her customers' comments, Barchetti also started to make more use of the database she had started to build up in the 1980s to customize and personalize her offerings to her customers. As a result of implementing her customers' suggestions, Barchetti has had an 8 per cent increase in profits, faster turnover of stock and more successful direct mail campaigns. A recent mail-out to 5000 customers, for instance, brought in 181 shoppers who spent $90,000 in one week, nearly doubling the usual level of sales for that calendar week.

I want to know our customers better than they know themselves.
Philip Condit, CEO, Boeing Aircraft

It is said that 80 percent of all successful new solutions come from customers' ideas.

What are your customers telling you? Are you listening?

Focus On Customer Satisfaction

Focusing on customer satisfaction is the first step to seeing the world from the customer's point of view. Satisfaction is the feeling people experience when their needs and expectations have been met. When they are exceeded we feel delighted. But when they are not — when reality is less than our expectation — we feel disappointed.

The greater the gap between reality and expectation, the greater the disappointment we feel. Most of us, especially males, become angry when we are disappointed. Anger energizes us to complain, either to the supplier who let us down

or, as is more usually the case, to everyone but the source of our dissatisfaction. Anger also drives us to take our business elsewhere.

In a tough market, you will be tempted to over-promise to attract business. Yet the more you promise, the harder it will be to satisfy your customers because you will have raised their expectations. This is known as the marketing paradox. Consultants who advise you to under-promise do not understand how competitive it is out there. You must raise your performance by developing better products and services, better systems and processes and, through better recruitment and training, better staff performance. You have no other alternative.

Customer satisfaction is not just something warm and fuzzy, it affects profitability. One hotel chain believes that a 1 per cent point increase in customer satisfaction brings in an extra US$60 million per year. One automobile manufacturer considers a one point increase in customer loyalty to be worth another US$100 million per year. And one airline company calculated that if they could put one extra person on each flight each day for one year it would bring in an extra US$ 115 million. How much would one more satisfied customer be worth to you? Do your people know this value?

Measure Customer Satisfaction

Every business leader knows how important customer satisfaction is and swears it is their most important goal. But, as with customer service, it is just not happening as it should be. Businesses promising to delight cannot even satisfy. A recent American study found that the majority of people quit using a law firm, for example, because they felt they were treated indifferently.

To make sure that you are living on the same planet as your customers, you must measure customer satisfaction. As the saying goes:

> *Without data, you're just another person with an opinion.*

I would suggest that a major customer survey once every one or two years is inadequate. A formal large-scale survey might be commissioned only once a year, but with smaller, more informal ways you should be sampling customer opinion at least once every two or three months, if not monthly. Mini-surveys and focus groups are good ways of getting to know your customers' needs and reactions.

How often do you measure your customers' satisfaction level? Which questions do you ask? Who do you give the results to? Do you compare your results to those of your competitors? What is done with this information?

It is important to talk to the right people. Often those asked have little direct experience with the supplier's performance and therefore cannot provide much useful information. Unhappy customers and customers that you have just lost should be surveyed because they will tell you what you need to do to improve. Prospective customers that you are having a hard time convincing to switch from their present supplier to you should be included because they will tell you how you can lift your game. But do not be like the hotel that a friend of mine went to. He is one of those people who is almost always happy, bubbly and positive. After he had breezed into the lobby to check out and brightened everyone up, the hotel clerk said: "You look like a happy customer. How would you like to complete one of our customer surveys for me?"

It is important to ask the right questions. Most customer surveys ask pretty lame questions, such as:

- *How well are we doing?*

- *Do you have any suggestions for how we can improve?*

They usually do not get much of a response because customers know the problems but do not know the answers. These companies then mistakenly interpret the lack of response as indicating the customer is satisfied when in reality it indicates only that they asked the wrong question.

Basically, you want to know the answer to ten questions:

1. *What do we do well that is important to you?*
   This is what you should **keep** doing.

2. *What do we do poorly that is important to you?*
   This is what you should **improve**.

3. *What do we do that you do not need?*
   This is what you should **stop** doing.

4. *What do we not do that you need us to do?*
   This is what you should **start** doing.

5. *What problems do you have satisfying your customers?*

6. *What problems do you have doing business with us?*
   The answers to Questions 5 & 6 are your **opportunities** to increase the value you create for your customers.

7. *Would you come back? If not, why not?*
   This will help you to improve **customer retention**.

8. *In what ways are we critical to your success?*
   This will help you to build a **partnership**.

9. *Would you recommend us to others? Why? Why not?*
   This will help you turn customers into **advocates**.

10. *How do we compare to your best supplier?*
   This will help you to **benchmark** your performance.

Once you have data about your customers' level of satisfaction, you need to do something with it. Companies spend large sums of money and valuable senior management time on customer satisfaction surveys and then do little that is meaningful with the results. Either they fail to study the results to find opportunities to improve, or they fail to pass on the results to their staff. Those that do, often fail to consult with their people to get their ideas about what could be changed to improve customer satisfaction. Other companies come up with good ideas and then fail to implement them. Great information, brilliant ideas and good decisions are worthless without action. It is not what you think about doing but what you actually do that will improve your business. If you are not going to act, do not bother doing the surveys in the first place. The road to ruin is paved with good intentions!

It is not what you think about doing, but what you actually do that will improve your business.

The first thing to do is to share the results with your entire staff. I mean everyone — part-timers included. Hold meetings to discuss the results. Celebrate the good results and problem-solve the poor ones. Be careful not to blame people for any bad news you get. Instead, look for problems with your policies, processes and procedures. Experience shows that the vast majority of performance problems are caused by faulty processes and only a few are caused by people.

Get your facts first, and then you are free to distort them as much as you please.
Mark Twain

The second thing to do is to compare your customer survey results with a) previous ones, to see if you are improving; and b) with those of your competitors. Cadillac thought it

Whose Side Are You On?

William Hewlett and Dave Packard built their successful company, Hewlett-Packard, by listening to their customers.

Noel Eldred, vice-president of marketing for H-P, was a strong advocate of seeing the customer's point of view — so much so that Eldred wanted his sales engineers to take the customer's side in any dispute with the company.

"We don't want you blindly agreeing with us," Eldred would tell his staff. "We want you to stick up for the customer. After all, we're not selling hardware, we're selling solutions to our customers' problems."

Eldred stressed the importance of listening to customer feedback and using it to design new products. He had the unqualified support of his fellow senior managers.

"We encourage every person in our organisation to think continuously about how his or her activities relate to the central purpose of serving our customers," says David Packard in his book, *The H-P Way*.

Whose side do you expect your people to be on?

Compare your cus-
tomer survey re-
sults with
a) previous ones,
to see if you are
improving; and
b) with those of
your competitors.

was doing just fine when it looked at its customer satisfaction figures. Then it started surveying potential customers and competitors' customers and found that the competition was getting better faster than they were.

Thirdly, identify some priorities and goals to work on between now and the next survey. Involve all staff to get their ideas and commitment. Frame your goals as action plans. In other words, outline *who* is going to do *what* by *when* — and decide when you are going to review progress. Do not set a large number of grandiose goals that are unlikely be achieved. Target a few important, realistic projects that *will* be accomplished. Then act. Just do something, and remember to measure the results.

Bring The Customer Into The Workplace

Over the past fifteen years I have tried many different approaches to enable staff to look through the eyes of the customer. By far the most powerful has been to call a staff meeting and invite real live customers. The more demanding and upset the customers, the better. Sometimes, we have invited customers the company upset so much they lost their business. On several occasions those customers have returned to the fold, saying to management: "If you are prepared to let me

come and tell your staff about what has been going wrong, then you must be serious about changing things around here. I'll give you another chance."

On other occasions we have invited people the company would liked to have had as customers but who, in spite of numerous approaches, have refused to shift from their existing supplier. In these cases, the company learns what it would have to be able to do to get them to switch. In some cases they do; but the primary benefit of these meetings is not marketing — it is to remove the barrier between customers and staff. Inadvertently, managers, marketers and sales people have become this barrier. They go out and talk to the customers and pass information back to "the troops", but because they have other agendas to follow, because they have developed poor relationships with front-line staff over the years, or because they are not good communicators, there is often a huge trust gap between the managers, marketers and sales people on the one hand, and front-line staff on the other. The conduit has turned into a brick wall and information that is essential to the success of the business is not getting through to those who need to hear it most.

Customer meetings are not difficult to organize and should be done regularly. The best time for the meetings is during normal working hours because that sends the message that learning about the customer is part of people's jobs, not something that is tacked on. Having said that, most staff will happily stay for an after-work meeting if they occur only two or three times a year, if they are interesting and fun (wine and pizzas are a good note to end on) and, most importantly, if they learn something and then later actually see things change.

It is always useful to involve an outside person to facilitate these customer meetings as both staff and customers will feel more comfortable speaking out if the sessions are not run by "the boss". The meeting should open with a statement from the business owner or CEO reaffirming the company's commitment to putting the customer first and stating their personal view about the importance of seeing the world through the customer's eyes. Next, one or two customers should be invited to speak for 10 or 15 minutes each. Brief them to

Ask your customers to describe what your business has done well for them over the past year and how that has helped them; and what things have gone wrong and the effects these snafus have had on their business.

describe what your business has done well for them over the past year and how that has helped them. Then ask them to describe what things have gone wrong and the effects these snafus have had on their business. Staff should be encouraged to ask questions to learn more about the customer's requirements, problems and view of their business. At this point, it is useful to break for a cup of coffee. This gives people a chance to chat to their customers and to digest what they have just heard. After the break and the customers have left, divide into small groups of eight to ten people and ask staff to discuss what they have learned about the:

- *Things which are important to the customer*

- *Things which we do well now*

- *Problems that have been identified*

- *Ideas they have for improvement*

After 30 to 45 minutes of discussion, the groups should report back and all ideas should be captured on a flip chart for future action. A good follow-up to these meetings is to arrange for a key customer to be interviewed on videotape each month. The tape can then be played at staff meetings.

Another good way to help people to see the customer's perspective is to use mystery shoppers. There are many companies which will send people into your business to interact with your staff and then provide a report on their experience. This is a good way of looking into the mirror. Recently I read an article in a Canadian newspaper where both business owners and their staff were against the use of mystery shoppers. They took the view that a mystery shopper was a spy out to get them. Using mystery shoppers is like a sports team watching videos of their last game, or dancers practicing in front of the mirror. We must learn to see ourselves as our customers see us. Theirs is the only view that matters.

Yet another idea is to send your staff out to visit your customers at their place of work to talk to them and to watch them use your products and services. Arrange for each work team to spend time with their opposite number. The team making industrial bags, for example, might spend half a day

We must learn to see ourselves as our customers see us. Theirs is the only view that matters.

Nine Steps To Holding Customer Meetings

1. Hold them during working hours.

2. Use an outside facilitator.

3. Invite two customers to speak for 15 minutes each about:
   - what you do well;
   - what you have done poorly;
   - how it has affected them.

4. Give people a chance to ask questions.

5. Have a coffee break.

6. Divide people into small, random groups of between seven and ten people to discuss:
   - what matters to our customers;
   - what do we do well;
   - what are the problems;
   - the ideas we have to improve.

7. Have the groups report back in a plenary session.

8. Compile their findings and give them to management.

9. Management: Do something with the information. Make sure both your customers and your staff see that you have done something with the information. Remember: Perception is reality!

Bringing the world of the customer into the workplace is one of the most important tasks for today's business leaders.

with the team who uses those bags, seeing the problems their customers have with them. It is also useful to organize return visits where your customer's staff come and spend time visiting your business. I have seen many good improvement ideas emerge from such visits.

Capture What You Learn

There are many ways that you can bring the world of the customer into the workplace. The important thing is that you do it. Think widely and bring in past and potential customers as well as current ones. Be daring. Invite your competitor's customer to come and speak to you! There is so much to gain that bringing the world of the customer into the workplace is one of the most important tasks of management today.

> *In business, you don't get rewarded by the boss for effort: you get rewarded by the customer for results.*

As you get to know your customers better and see what they see, you will learn valuable lessons. Do not waste them. Become a learning organisation. Invest money in understanding things about your customers and then record them so they can be used in the future.

Since customers are your business, the more you know about your customers the more you will know about your business. The next step is to use this knowledge to make your customers successful.

Summary

- **Value exists in the eyes of the beholder.** We must learn to look through our customers' eyes.

- **Are you making your business work for your customers** or your customers work for your business? If your profit targets and internal business systems become more important than the customer, you will end up serving yourself and not your customers. Your customers will end up going elsewhere.

- **What do your customers see?** Is your business customer-friendly? Are your staff friendly? How about your signs? How easy it is for your customers to do business with you? Get inside your customer's skin.

- **Get the culture right.** Change people's behaviour. Transform your employees into business people. Require your staff to spend some time every week working in teams to systematically understand more about their customers — be they internal or external.

- **Seek answers from your customers.** If you watch closely and listen carefully, your customers will tell you everything you need to know to run a successful business.

- **Measure customer satisfaction.** Get hard data, share it with your staff, compare yourself to your competitors and use the information to drive improvement activity. Make changes. Act.

- **Bring the world of the customer into the workplace.** Theirs is the only point of view that matters. Make sure that people hear it, think about it and act on it.

- **Capture what you have learned.** You have gone to a lot of trouble to learn about your customer and their view of the world, you should capture it so it is available to everyone at anytime, now or in the future.

- **The more you know** about your customers, the more you will know about your business. Now use this information to make your customers successful.

How Are *You* Doing?

In which ways do you make your customers
work for your business?

In which ways do you look out at the world from inside
your business?

What are the risks doing this?

What steps do you take to see the world from your
customers' perspectives?

What would your front-line staff say about what your
customers think of your service?

What would your customers say?

How customer-friendly is your business?

How friendly are your signs?

How friendly are your staff?

How easy are you to do business with?

Are your policies customer-focused?

Are your staff competent?

How do you handle customer complaints?

How would your staff describe your culture?

Who would your staff say they work for?

What is your vision? Does your vision statement describe the value you aim to add to your customers?

Are your management decisions in agreement with your policy of putting the customers first?

Do you give your staff the tools they need to put the customer first?

What are you doing to transform your employees into business people?

What are your strategies for seeking answers from your customers?

• How often do you measure customer satisfaction?

• What do the results tell you?

• Do you compare your results to those of your competitors?

• Who do you give the results to?

• What is done with this information?

Now, be honest. Have you answered these questions as the supplier, or as your customers might answer them? Would your customers agree with your answers? How do you know?

How do you involve your staff in finding ways to increase customers' satisfaction?

What are you going to change to serve your customers better?

How would you rate your track record in implementing changes? (circle one)

Very poor   Poor   Average   Good   Excellent

How do you capture what you have learned about your customers and keep it for future use?

Do you encourage staff to find innovative ways to solve customer's problems? Do you give them the necessary authority? Do you reward them for doing this?

✸ Strategy 4

Make Your Customers Successful

Although customer service is important in this crowded market, servicing or even satisfying your customers is not enough, because customers who are "merely satisfied" defect to other suppliers at an alarmingly high rate. If you want to be second to none, you must work to make your customers successful.

Making your customers successful means understanding what they are trying to accomplish and then helping them to do it. Follow the philosophy that if your customers win, then you will win. Look after their interests first.

Begin by selecting the customer groups you wish to serve and then work to build a strong relationship with them. Be aware that relationships go through stages. Develop your key relationships to the point where your customers trust you.

Next, become part of their business. Talk to your customer's customers to see what you can do to help your customers satisfy their customers. If you help your customers to succeed, they will want to become your partner, giving you customer loyalty and repeat business. They might even become your advocates and tell others how much value you have provided to them.

Anything that you can do to help your customers succeed, they will value. It is as simple as that. On the other hand, if you let your customers down, you make it very difficult for them to satisfy their customers. The more you are able to understand what your customers are trying to do, the more opportunities you will find to help them — and yourself.

High level and long-term customer satisfaction is attainable if a company focuses on it, is responsive to customer demands and is constantly innovative.

Customer Service Is Important

Customer service is both a promise and an activity, but there is often a gap between what we promise and what we do. Failure to focus on customer service can force a business to focus on failure, as Xerox discovered in the early 1980s. Xerox, when it was a small photo-paper firm called Haloid, agreed to produce Chester Carlson's photocopying machine, and for twenty years they owned both the technology and the market. Xerox was unbeatable, but during their years of dominance they became complacent about product quality, customer service and innovation. Then the Japanese entered the market and by 1981 Xerox had lost over 50 per cent of its market share and 50 per cent of its profits. In response, CEO David Kearns refocused the company on the customer. From 1985 to 1989 Xerox's customer satisfaction level increased 38 per cent. Encouraged by this, Xerox set a goal for 1990 to get ratings of "satisfied" or "very satisfied" from 90 per cent of its 2.2 million customers. The goal was increased in 1991 to 94 per cent and in 1993 to 100 per cent! Most CEOs would consider 100 per cent customer satisfaction to be unrealistic, but some divisions within Xerox achieved that target as early as 1990 and have maintained customer satisfaction at that level ever since. Xerox has shown that high level and long-term customer satisfaction is attainable if a company focuses on it, is responsive to customer demands and is constantly innovative.

Some Good Things Are Happening

Certainly you can encounter some very good examples of superb customer service, like the experience I had with Koru Valet Parking at Auckland airport (described in *The Yellow Brick Road*). There are also some very good customer-focused companies in addition to Xerox, such as the American retailer, Nordstrom, whose customer service is legendary. Staff will accept returns on merchandise bought at another store, run off to the airport with a just-altered dress or tell a customer the less expensive item of clothing actually suits them better. Another service star is Toyota's Lexus Division whose service standard is to treat each customer as one would treat a guest in one's home.

Even some small business operators are catching on. In Chicago, at a fast food outlet at O'Hare Airport, my eye was caught by a display of pictures of staff who had excelled. These were not called employees of the month but Customer Service Leaders. Recently, I took a taxi in Toronto and the cabby gave me a number of daily papers to read and asked me what kind of music I would like to listen to on the radio. When my family moved to a new city in Canada, my wife opened an account at Scotia Bank. A week later, the bank officer who had handled the new account telephoned to see if there was anything she could do to help us settle in to the city.

> *In today's business battles, customer service is the secret weapon.*
> Robert McDermott,
> former CEO, USAA

There are countless other examples of people delivering excellent service. On the other hand, it is also very easy to experience poor customer service on a daily basis. What is disturbing is that the managers of many of those businesses delivering poor service believe their company is doing a great job of looking after their customers. As someone once said: "It's not what you don't know that causes problems in life. It's what you 'know' that ain't necessarily so!" This is especially a problem in large companies where senior management is removed from the coal-face.

> *Very big companies don't know a goddamn thing about customer service. They know about financing and delivering goods, but they haven't the faintest clue of what it is to wait on customers.*
> Stanley Marcus,
> Chairman Emeritus,
> Neiman Marcus Group

But working hard to deliver good customer service, although important, is not enough if you aim to become second to none. Focusing on customer service makes it easy to fall into the trap of looking from the inside out and, as a result,

Five Steps To Managing Your Way To Excellent Customer Service

Do not just send front-line staff on customer service training courses. Send managers and supervisors to learn how to:

1. Hire the right kind of people.

2. Bring the world of the customer into the workplace.

3. Train and motivate staff to deliver good service.

4. Reward staff for delivering outstanding service.

5. Create a culture of enthusiasm for caring about the customer and delivering value.

delivering a service that the customer does not want. Even if you manage to get it right, you run the risk of not seeing un-tapped service opportunities. At least if you raise your sights and focus on customer satisfaction you will be forced to start with the customer's view of the world. You must understand their needs and monitor whether your actions are having the desired affect. Customer service is what you do. Customer satisfaction is what your customers think about what you do. And there can be a big difference between the two.

Customer service is what you do. Customer satisfaction is what your customers think about what you do.

Satisfying Your Customers Is Not Enough

But perhaps your business is one of those that is able to satisfy its customers. Is that enough in this challenging marketplace? The answer is a resounding "No!"

With all the choices they have available to them, customers defect at an alarming rate. Every year, more than 50 per cent of customers in the cable TV market discontinue their service, while cellular telephone companies lose 30–45 per cent of their customers, and in the remote pager business the loss rate can be as high as 70 per cent a year. Banks and insurance companies have long recognized that their customers are not very loyal because they see little difference between one supplier and the next. A study by Market Vision 2000, for instance, found that 64 per cent of Canadians polled regarded all banks as being the same. Customer defections should worry you too, because loyal customers are your future. Studies show that 80 per cent of the purchases made in any given business come from repeat customers.

Repeat business is like compounding interest.
S. Todd Burns

Myths About Customer Loyalty

Myth 1 Customer defection is beyond your control. A small percentage of customers will always go elsewhere.

Myth 2 Customer service is the job of front-line employees only.

Myth 3 Complaints are bad news.

Myth 4 Only dissatisfied customers defect.

Research is revealing just how important those long-term customers are to profitability. A study of banking in the USA found that although long-term customers comprised only 29 per cent of a bank's business, they produced 71 per cent of the profit. Some experts believe there is a 5 to 1 net revenue advantage to having loyal customers. Others say that if companies increase their customer retention by 2 per cent, it is equivalent to cutting their operating costs by 10 per cent. I read recently in the *Harvard Business Review* that increasing your customer retention by 5 per cent can lead to profit increases of up to 80 per cent.

Another banking study showed just how much business is lost by ignoring the potential of a partnership. The Royal Bank of Canada discovered a few years ago that each of their customers purchased, on average, 75 financial products during the course of their lifetimes. What concerned the Royal Bank was that those customers purchased only three from them. Today, the bank pays less attention to recruiting new customers and puts more effort into getting their existing customers to purchase more of their products.

Loyal customers, then, are an economic asset. They provide higher profits, repeat business and higher market share. They are also an important source of new referrals. A customer base takes time, money and effort to build but it is the source of future cash flow. Costs that are incurred in growing that customer base should be considered an investment. Your customer base must be carefully managed like any other asset and if you are not measuring customer retention, you are probably not managing it.

Most companies have higher than desired rates of customer defection, but what is even more alarming is that customers who defect are not always unhappy. According to research conducted by Bain & Company in the United States, 65 to 85 per cent of customers who desert their supplier and take their business elsewhere are either satisfied or very satisfied customers at the time they switch. Some experts believe that up to 40 per cent of your existing satisfied customers will go to a competitor. Why are customers so fickle? Because most people today have very high standards of supplier performance.

> *Costs that are incurred in growing your customer base should be considered to be an investment.*

> *More and more companies have come to realize that placing an inordinate emphasis on drumming up new business is costly and often detrimental. The real money is to be made selling to the customers you already have. In fact, having high customer retention is often a much more valuable index of an enterprise's health than its ability to bring in new customers. Because if you have high customer retention, you are getting, by definition, plenty of new business.*
>
> James Champy, Sales & Marketing Manager, January, 1997

*Customers who de-
fect are not always
unhappy. Between
65 and 85 per cent
of those customers
who desert their
supplier and take
their business else-
where are either
satisfied or very sat-
isfied customers.*

They expect to be satisfied and when they are it is no big deal. Satisfying your customers is not enough. Something more is required to keep customers loyal.

A study of banking done by the Juran Institute in America found that people who rated their bank as "outstanding" were four times less likely to defect to a competitor. These people were also five times more likely to go out and buy another financial service from their bank. In this world full of well-educated, sophisticated and demanding customers, business success comes from doing more than merely satisfying your customers. You have to work to make them successful.

Make Your Customers Successful

Imagine one of your customers wanted you to do something for them. If you wanted to satisfy them, you would eagerly do what they asked. But suppose you wanted to make them successful. Before you acted on their request you would probably say: "Look, I am happy to do as you ask but before I do let me ask you a silly question, why do you want me to do that?" Then, after hearing their answer and having learned something about their needs, you might find yourself saying: "Well, if that's what you want to achieve, I could do what you asked but it would be faster or cheaper if we did this instead."

*Your customers are
trying to do the
same thing as you
are trying to do
and that is to be
successful in their
own business or
personal life.*

Five Steps to Making Your Customers Successful

1. Follow the philosophy that if your customers win then you will win.

2. Be clear on who your key customers are.

3. Build relationships with your customers.

4. Become part of your customer's business.

5. Talk to your customer's customers.

To focus on customer satisfaction is to be reactive and passive, and it can mean missing opportunities to create value. Customers often do not say what they mean or mean what they say. To get it right, you need to be proactive, probing and creative. Striving to make your customers successful will cause you to do that. A camera manufacturer discovered this in the 1970s when single lens reflex cameras (SLR) were all the rage. While other manufacturers concentrated on finding ways of making better SLR cameras, one company started asking questions that led it to realise that people do not want good cameras — they want good pictures. By studying typical faults in people's photographs, this heads-up company developed fully automatic point and shoot cameras with a built-in flash. They not only captured a huge chunk of the market, they redefined their industry.

Concentrating on making your customers successful will cause you to be probing, proactive and creative.

Another reason for making your customers successful is that they fear failure. Every commercial customer worries that their supplier will let them down, putting them in a position of letting their own customers down as a result. I stayed in a five-star hotel when launching my last book. The hotel was hosting the book launch and spared no effort to treat me royally. After the launch I had a meeting in my suite with a prospective client. I offered my guest a cup of coffee but when I added the milk I saw it had gone sour. I phoned the concierge and explained the situation. He said a new carton of milk would be sent right up. I apologized to my prospective client and said new milk was on the way. It never came. Does that failure to serve simply cause me to be dissatisfied? No, it threatens my business because of how it makes me look in the eyes

Your poor performance can put your customer out of business. Then where will you be?

of my customer. Especially since the theme of the book was quality management!

Your performance scares your customers to death because when things go wrong their customers will blame them and not you. They may lose customers and may even go out of business as a result of your actions. But there is an upside to this customer paranoia. It provides an opportunity for you to create value. Anything you can do to help your customers satisfy their customers, they will love you for. As a result, they will value your reliability and your contribution to their own business success.

The First Step

If You Win, I Win

The first step to making your customers successful is to follow the philosophy that if your customers win then you will win. This is the opposite from what most businesses seem to be saying to their customers. For example, downtown parking lots where the attendants demand a deposit before you can leave your car there are really saying:

> *Since a small percentage of my customers will try
> to cheat me, I will treat everyone as a potential crook
> because what is most important is that I win.*

Customers do not like this attitude. They expect to be treated with dignity and respect. Moreover, when it appears that your primary focus is to look out for yourself, it makes them nervous. This increases their exposure to risk because they cannot be confident that you will put their interests first.

Make your customers successful and you will make yourself successful. Some companies appear to understand this very well. Harry Bullis, former Chairman of General Mills, used to encourage his sales people to go out and help as many people as possible by telling them: "He who goes out to help his fellow man to a happier and easier way of life is exercising the highest type of salesmanship."

An example of a service provider who did not follow Bullis's

He who goes out to help his fellow man to a happier and easier way of life is exercising the highest type of salesmanship.

Harry Bullis

102

advice can be found in a well-known story about golfer Arnold Palmer. It seems Palmer was having dinner with his lawyer in a fancy restaurant one evening. The lawyer was not happy with the service they received and made a big scene in the restaurant. Afterwards, Palmer took his lawyer aside and expressed his displeasure: "I did not like your behaviour in the restaurant this evening. I don't behave like that myself and I don't want people to think that I ever would. When you behave that way and people see us together, they think that I condone it. Next time we are out together, please behave as I would."

If you worry more about your customer's competitors than your own, you will end up being more competitive yourself. As Eli Goldratt, author of *The Goal* and the proponent of the theory of restraint, says: "We cannot just give the customers what they want, we should also be in a position to give them what they really need — which will help them to reach their goal."

Some companies reflect this *"If you win, I win"* philosophy in their vision statements; whereas those of others are self-serving. While the *"We're looking out for us first"* group are driven by such lofty purposes as:

- *To be the most preferred supplier*

- *To be rated number one in our market*

- *To have the biggest market share*

Those who put their customers first, as we saw in Strategy 1 (see page 16), have more noble aims:

- *To democratize the automobile (Ford)*

- *To give unlimited opportunities to women (Mary Kay)*

- *To preserve and improve human life (Merck)*

Many companies let their advertising show their commitment to making their customers successful. AT&T, for example, advertises:

> *Until now, your customers outside North America had to pay every time they called your 800 number. Today that barrier to global business comes down.*

Profit is the result of doing some very special work — and that special work involves putting your customers' interests ahead of your own.

103

General Electric's Capital Services claims:

> *"Our business is helping yours to see what your competition can't."*

Or JP Morgan states:

> *"Creating value is your ultimate goal. That's why you call JP Morgan."*

And MassMutual, a financial services company, announces:

> *"For more than 140 years, we've been helping people keep their promises (to their families)."*

However you communicate your intention to put your customer's success first, remember that what is most important is that you truly believe in the *"If you win, I win"* philosophy. Jim Penman is an example of a business leader who does. In 1989, Penman started a lawn mowing business called Jim's Mowing, which by 1992 was the fastest growing franchise business in Australia. Today there are Jim's Mowing franchisees throughout Australia, New Zealand and in parts of Canada and the United States. In fact, Jim's Mowing is the largest lawn-mowing franchise company in the world. How did a man with a grub stake of A$25 become so successful in a crowded business like lawn-mowing?

Unlike many people who try to franchise their businesses, Penman put his franchisee's success ahead of his own. This is unusual. In my experience, many franchisors treat their franchisees as if they, not the competition, were the enemy. I have heard them speak about their franchisees in a derogatory way and use them as scapegoats when things go wrong. Most alarmingly, some franchisors take the view that the success of their franchisees comes at their own expense — as if successful franchisees are cheating them somehow. Penman, on the other hand, took the view that if he was to succeed his franchisees must succeed first. He saw his franchisees as being his customers and did whatever he had to do to make it possible for them to satisfy their customers. His reward was a successful business. Of course, Jim was not the first to do this. Ray Kroc, the founder of the McDonald's Corporation, also had that focus. At a time when most fast food franchisors were taking advantage of every opportunity to charge their franchisees, Kroc took the view that first he must help his franchisees to succeed.

The Second Step

Identify Your Key Customers

Once you are clear in your mind that you will put your customers first, you must be clear on who your key customers are — or who you would like to them to be. This is the fundamental issue everyone should ask themselves before they set up in business and should review at least annually as part of their strategic planning. Ask these two questions:

- *What business are we in?*

- *Who is our target market?*

These are not easy questions to answer. Indeed, you could spend you entire working life trying to come up with the "right" answer. Struggle with them, because the answers define your business. They will help you to develop successful competitive strategies and to focus your precious resources more effectively.

There is so much work that has to be done with customers that you could not possibly do it with all of them unless you had huge resources and very sophisticated technology. *Air Miles* and *Fly Buys.* programmes are designed to collect very detailed information about the buying patterns of individual consumers within a huge market, but these are recent developments. It is now also possible for small businesses to build effective databases, thanks to modern technology and some excellent business software. But it takes time to do and you are best advised to concentrate on those key 20 per cent of your customers who will generate 80 per cent of your sales. Get to know them. Spend time with them and with their customers to learn all you can about what you can do to make them successful. Find out everything from how much money they have to what they are afraid of most. Find out how their business systems work and then design your ordering and invoicing systems to be compatible with them. Find out how

Ask yourself, which customers can we serve best to our mutual benefit over a long period of time?

often they like to be called, want to order and want to be billed. What are their pet loves and hates? If they like voice mail, make it available to them. If they want to talk to a real live human being, make that possible, too. Build a strong relationship with them. Make your knowledge of their business, your concern about their success and your friendship what differentiates you from your competition.

Because of the difficulties and the time involved in getting close to a large number of customers, the trend in retailing and in most business areas is that you must be very big and dominate your category or you must occupy a very small niche. Thus, The Warehouse and the Pacific Retail Group in New Zealand or K-Mart and Myers in Australia, have become "category killers" in their areas, and other stores are scurrying to find a niche for themselves. More and more walk-in medical clinics are popping up, and the neighbourhood family doctor is left to find a reason to exist. To differentiate themselves, sole practitioners in professions such as medicine, law and dentistry must find a niche to occupy that makes them different from everyone else, particularly the large nationwide practices. This is true for nearly all businesses. Large companies that once dominated their market and successfully co-existed with one or two competitors now find themselves locked in fierce "fight-to-the-death" battles with several equally large competitors. At the same time, the rats and mice are nibbling away at the edge of their business, often picking the eyes out of it and leaving them with the high-cost, low-margin trade.

This trend towards niche markets is partly driven by globalization and partly by more sophisticated customers who know that you cannot be all things to all people and are suspicious if you claim to be. It is also due to a more complex society where, since no one person or group can know everything, the star of the generalist is waning and that of the specialist is rising. As Aristotle Onassis, the shipping magnate, once said: "The key to business is to know something no one else knows."

Many business people are beginning to discover large untapped markets and huge business opportunities as they specialise. These entrepreneurs are realizing that many potential

Sales forces that are thriving in today's marketplace aren't just adapting to the needs of customers — they're investing time and energy in the right customers.
James Champy, Co-author,
Re-engineering the Corportation

customers have never understood the value their businesses can offer because these customers have not been targeted and the value proposition (benefits less costs) has not been presented. A good rule to keep in mind is "The smaller the niche, the bigger the market".

The more you specialize in a particular market group, the more you will learn about their problems and the more you will see opportunities to create value by solving those problems. But it is difficult to get to know strangers. This brings us to the third step for making your customers successful, building a strong relationship with them.

Rule: The smaller the niche, the bigger the market.

Remember, though, that your future business success comes from the future — not the present and certainly not the past. Invest some time in strategic thinking. Who are going to be your key customers in the future? What problems will they be trying to solve and what will they need from you? How will you have to be able to reshape your business to provide your future customers with the solutions they will be seeking?

The Third Step

Build Relationships

You will get the knowledge you need to understand your customer's business thoroughly only if your customer trusts you, and they will trust you only if you have developed a good relationship with them. Building this relationship is the third step to making your customers successful. The key word here is build. Relationships take work. They do not just happen. You have to want to build the relationship badly enough to put the hard work and time into it. You have to show genuine interest in your customers and convince them that you care about them. We do not usually bond with people who do not care about us.

Building relationships is also not easy. The path to building good relationships is littered with frustrations, misunderstandings and conflicts. Good communication is essential. What is more, the work does not stop when the relationship is built. As anyone who is married knows, it takes more work to maintain a relationship than it did to build it in the first place.

Never during my visit did she (the store clerk) ask me how much money I wanted to spend, who my favourite designers were… or what fashion pet peeves I had.
A customer quoted in *Fortune* 11/12/95

It is interesting to think that there are roughly five and one half billion people on this planet and nearly all of them live and work in a network of social relationships. We may speak different languages, have different physical characteristics, follow different customs and believe in different religions but we are all the same in our need to relate to others. In fact, I know of no society where it is considered normal to live and work in total isolation. To be a hermit is to be abnormal, unusual, deviant.

So why is it that we live in this network of social relationships? Think about yourself. Why do you live in relationships? What do you personally get from the relationships you live in? These may be questions you have asked yourself a lot lately! If you list all of the things you get out of your relationships you might find yourself thinking about such things as love, security, belonging, achievement and support. These are basic human needs. We relate to others to get our needs met. Some of you may have listed happiness, contentment and satisfaction

Who Are Your Key Customers?
(And what do you know about them?)

- List them by name or by group.

- Where do they live?

- What jobs do they have?

- What is their income?

- Which hobbies and interests do they have?

- Which cars do they like to drive?

- What do they watch on TV?

- Which books, magazines and newspapers do they read?

- How do they spend their disposable income?

- What do they do in their spare time?

- What are their dreams?

- What are their fears?

- Who makes the buying decisions in the family?

- How do they arrive at that decision?

as things you get from your relationships. These are feelings we get when our needs are met. Whether it is a social situation or a commercial transaction, the psychology is the same: People enter into relationships to get their needs met and when they do, they feel satisfied.

This human part of the commercial transaction is very important. So much so that I seriously doubt that home shopping from the TV or the Internet is likely to dominate retailing or the provision of services such as financial planning and insurance. The electronic media are fine for order-taking, but when it comes to making the buying decision, customers need the security of working within a social relationship. Without the relationship, there is no trust and the emotional cost becomes too high. Merrill Lynch understands this. They sell advice, analysis and expertise through 12,000 financial consultants at retail offices throughout the USA. Says William Henkel, head of market planning in the private client division: "We absolutely believe that a person's financial security is too complex for an 0800 number."

People become involved in relationships to get their needs met and when they do, they feel satisfied. If they do not, they will try to leave the relationship.

When people find themselves in a relationship where their needs are met, they will be motivated to work to strengthen that relationship. On the other hand, if they are not getting their needs met, they will want to end it. Loyal customers are those whose needs are met so well they want to stick with that supplier. To them the idea of switching is scary and it cannot be outweighed by a slightly lower price.

$$Trust = \frac{Behaviour - Expectation}{Time}$$

Trust is an important part of relationships. It is also not a very well understood concept. Like most powerful ideas, it is quite a simple one. Trust is simply your behaviour minus the customer's expectation over time. Imagine that you expected me to give you $10. If I gave you $10 or more, you would trust me to keep my word next time. But if I gave you $9 or less, you would begin to doubt me. The longer this went on, the more you would doubt me. The conclusion is clear. If you want people to trust you, do what you say you are going to do. It is that simple. The corollary is that time is on your side, but only as long as you are meeting your customer's expectations. The longer a customer is with you, the stronger your relationship will become, providing trust is being developed. In the banking industry studies show that 26 per cent of new customers defect in the first year but by year nine only 9 per cent switch to another supplier.

Relationships go through stages. The first stage is the romance stage or honeymoon period. Some of you may remember this starry-eyed time where everything and everyone is wonderful, thanks to the rose-coloured glasses you are wearing. This near-mystical state exists because we look at the new person, house, job or deodorant and expect that by getting involved with it we will get our needs met. In boy-girl type relationships, scientific studies show the romance stage has a shelf life of 18 to 24 months. I do not know how long it lasts in commercial relationships but I suspect quite a bit less. Enjoy the time when your new customer is besotted with you by all means, but do not bask in it too long. It is only puppy love and the relationship will disappear very quickly unless you work at it.

The longer a customer is with you, the stronger your relationship will become providing trust is being developed.

The Stages Of Relationships

Stage One: **The Honeymoon Period**
It lasts 18 to 24 months. It feels wonderful but it is all illusion.

Stage Two: **The Power Struggle**
Win/Lose Conflict. Even if you win, you lose because the customer will go elsewhere.

Stage Three: Acceptance
You accept the customer's needs are just as important as your own and you put them first.

Stage Four: Cooperation
You work together with your customer to achieve a win for both of you.

Stage Five: Stability
Customer loyalty is the reward for having worked to build a strong relationship.

The second stage, into which one inevitably drifts no matter what the relationship, is the power struggle. This is not really a struggle for power. It is a struggle to use whatever power you can lay your grubby little hands on to get your needs met. You, as the supplier, can never win this struggle, although as a customer I have personally dealt with many who thought they could. Maybe you are right about the facts and the customer has it all wrong. Maybe the customer should have read the contract better. Maybe the law is on your side. At the end of the day, if the customer does not get their needs met they will take their business elsewhere and you lose. There is probably not a lot of satisfaction in being right but broke.

Stage three is the acceptance stage. This is where you accept that the other person's needs are just as important as your own. They may be different to your needs, but they are just as valid. If you follow the *"If you win, I win"* philosophy outlined previously, then you will be doing this. The acceptance stage is a pivotal one. Conflict is a natural part of human life because people have different needs. Most people open with a position statement such as:

> *I'm returning this coat I bought but I don't have the receipt.*

What the customer is really saying if you decode it is:

> *I have a need to return this coat but I am worried you won't take it back because I lost the receipt. I'll be in trouble with my partner if I cannot get my money back.*

But what the store clerk thinks is:

> *If I let the customer return this coat and give them their money back without a receipt, I will be in big trouble with the boss.*

So, the store clerk says:

> *Sorry, you cannot return it without the receipt.*

Both parties hear that the two positions are mutually exclusive because the customer cannot return the coat and not return the coat at the same time. Only one will win. They are in the power struggle stage and will fight to the death.

How do you get from the customer's position statement to win/win? You listen. You learn to decode what the customer is saying and you communicate acceptance. Remember, the key to listening is to accept what the other person has to say. You do not have to like it. You do not have to understand it. You do not have to agree with it. And you do not have to know what to do about it. You just have to accept that that is their point of view and they are entitled to it.

To get into the acceptance stage, instead of a position statement, the clerk would acknowledge the customer's problem and then outline their own.

> *I can tell it is important to you to return the coat and I want to let you do that. My problem is that if I give you your money back without having proof of purchase the boss will have me for lunch.*

Now we have two problems on the table. Both have been acknowledged and accepted as valid problems. You are ready to move into stage four, the cooperation stage where both parties work together to solve both of their problems — to gain a win/win. The first thing you must do is add the two problems together. Remember, you are trying to solve both your problem and your customer's. It must be very apparent to your customer that you are keen to solve their problem if you want to have their cooperation. Next, you must look for all the options you can find to solve that combined problem. Problem solving is a matter of probabilities. The more alternatives you can think of, the greater the chance you will find a solution that works.

Cooperation involves negotiating, and negotiation is the art of the possible. You must give and take. Accept right from the beginning that you will not get your preferred option or there would have been no conflict in the first place. Abandon that dream and start to look for options you can live with. Think about what is most important to you and try to get it. Think about what is least important to you and give it up. Try to figure out what is most important to your customer and let them have it. Find out what does not matter so much to them. Use the language of negotiation: two small but powerful words,

Getting To Win/Win

Negotiation is the art of the possible.

How do you get from the customer's position statement to win/win?

You listen.

You learn to decode what the customer is saying and you communicate acceptance.

The key to listening is to accept what the other person has to say.
• You do not have to like it.
• You do not have to understand it.
• You do not have to agree with it.
• You do not have to know what to do about it.

You just have to accept that that is their point of view and they are entitled to it.

You must communicate to your customer that you accept their need and that you care about them being able to get that need met.

Show them that you will work to solve their problem. Then use your problem-solving skills and find a solution that will work well for them and is acceptable to you.

"if" and "then". For example, the clerk could say:

> **If** *you would write your name, address, telephone number and the date you purchased the coat,* **then** *I will refund your money in full."*

These are very good words to use in negotiations because they are bi-lateral. They do not involve either of you giving up anything unless you both agree so they allow you to explore options without fear of losing. Remember, you cannot afford to have anything less than a very satisfied customer because even they defect. You should be aiming for a delighted customer and for that to happen your customer will need to see that they got something extra with no added cost (see Strategy 6). Your customer will need to see that you gave up more than they did.

To be delighted, your customer will need to see that you gave up more than they did.

If you cooperate over a long enough period of time in your relationship, you will move into the fifth stage, which is stability. This is the secure and comfortable feeling you both

Six Steps To Achieve A Win/Win

1. Work to solve both your problem and your customer's. Add the two problems together to form one combined problem that must be solved for you both to be happy.

2. Look for all the options you can find to solve that combined problem. Problem solving is a matter of probabilities. The more alternatives you can think of, the greater the chance you will find a solution that works.

3. Be prepared to give and take. Negotiation is the art of the possible. Accept from the beginning that you will not get your preferred option.

4. Start to look for options you can live with. What is most important to you? Go for it. What is least important to you? Give it up. What is most important to your customer? Let them have it. What does not matter so much to them that you can take?

5. Use the language of negotiation: "If... then."

6. Agree on something. Remember, you cannot afford to have anything less than a very satisfied customer.

have that, even if something does go wrong and there is conflict, you will sort it out to your mutual satisfaction. This is the partnership stage when the pay-off for you is customer loyalty, customer retention and lots of repeat business.

In business, you may not have the luxury of beginning in the honeymoon phase because customers will bring their past experience with other suppliers with them and transfer their bad feelings from them to you. You may, therefore, find yourself starting off in the power struggle. The way out is to listen to your customer. By listening to their concerns and trying to understand their point of view (see Strategy Three), you will convey acceptance and pave the way for you to move into the cooperation phase. No one said it would be easy, but it is worth the effort.

Relationships are dynamic. Just as customers' expectations change over time, so do relationships. Once built, the relationship with your customer will require constant work and attention. Customers are always thinking, "What have you done for me lately?"

Relationships change. Customers are always thinking, "What have you done for me lately?"

Relationships also involve everyone from the CEO to the youngest recruit. A relationship may start out as a single contact between a salesperson and a buyer, but it strengthens as connections are made between CEOs, and between staff in shipping and receiving, invoicing and accounts payable, and those who make the product and those who use it. What you need is everyone in the company asking themselves daily, "What can I do to grow this relationship?" because relationships either get stronger or they get weaker. If you do nothing to expand the number of connections between your company and your customer's and if you do nothing to strengthen each connection, the relationship will eventually wither and die.

One last word about relationships. Always remember that commercial relationships are really just social relationships. After all, business takes place between people. Your company cannot relate to IBM. When you build a relationship with your customer, make it personal. Let them get to know you as a person and try to get to know them as individuals. It is sometimes hard to believe but these people are not just "more bloody customers" sent by the devil to make your life impossible.

They are human beings who have the same needs, feelings and thoughts as you do. Treat them as you would like to be treated. Work towards developing a personal bond with your customers. If your customers have a choice between two sales people selling equivalent products or services, they will spend their time and their money with the one with whom they have the best social relationship.

The Fourth Step

Become Part Of Their Business

To make your customers successful, you must understand two things:

1. your industry — its products, services, processes and technology;
2. your customer's business.

Clearly, if you are not competent in your field neither you nor your customers will succeed. Perhaps there was a time when you could compete to win by being knowledgeable only about your industry, but not today. If you build a better mouse trap, the world will not beat a path to your door. Ask any marketer! If you aim to be second to none, you must know not only what your customers need, you must know it better than they do. The fourth step to making your customers successful is to become part of their business.

The fourth step to making your customers successful is to become part of their business.

You have to work to create what Fred Wiersema, co-author of *The Discipline of Market Leaders,* calls customer intimacy. In his recent book, called — not surprisingly — *Customer Intimacy*, Wiersema says companies must go beyond selling to get involved in their customer's business to help them get better results. You do this by getting to know your customer's business almost as well as you know your own.

One way of getting to know your customer's business is to send staff to spend time with your customers. Abitibi-Price, the Can$2.8 billion, 8000 employee, Canadian pulp and paper company, developed what they call *Customer Value Teams* in 1992. The teams' job is to go into the world of their customers and learn more about their business. They try, for example, to understand the most suitable kind of stock advertisers want newspapers to use. Similarly, Sandra Wilkin built a successful construction company in New York City specializing in building and renovating facilities for doctors and hospitals. A nurse by training, Wilkin once saw a contractor make some serious mistakes which both cost the contractor money and upset the doctor-customer because the contractor did not understand the doctor's business. Wilkin saw the opportunity to use her professional training to build a successful construction business. According to Wilkin, the real key to her success, however, was not her nursing expertise but that she spent time understanding her customer's business: "What we wound up doing was spending a lot of time with the client and understanding their business. That's different from someone who may have had the experience but didn't think it was necessary to spend that quality time with the client."

The aim of spending time with your customer is not to talk and sell but to listen and learn. Help your customers identify the causes of their performance problems and ask them what problems they have satisfying their customers. Observe their processes at work and talk not just to management but to shop-floor and front-line people as well. All the time you should look for an overlap between your customers' needs, what you do best and what you really enjoy doing. This is your niche, your area of competitive advantage (see page 118). For example, Nypro Inc. of Massachusetts (USA), a company that makes plastic parts by injection moulding, found that some companies in the medical field had problems making products with the necessary degree of precision. Nypro designed unique processes for each customer to give them the precision parts they needed to manufacture their products. The result was that sales quadrupled while profits grew more than thirteenfold.

The aim of spending time with your customer is not to talk and sell but to listen and learn.

The World's Shortest Sales Course

1. Know your customer's business.

2. Know your stuff.

Take such damn good care of your customers that they have no choice but to do business with you.

Guy Kawasaki, *How to Drive Your Competition Crazy*

117

When you talk to your customers, try to identify work they have to do to operate their businesses but which is adding no value for their customers. Can you take that work over? Can you look after stock-take and re-ordering? Can you manage their document system rather than just sell photcopying machines? How about machine inspection and minor preventative maintenance? Bearings Inc., an American manufacturer of ball bearings, does energy audits of the motors of its major industrial customers. People in the distribution business see an increasing overlap between their usual functions and those of their customers. Supervalue Inc., a US$12.6 billion wholesaler, helps its retail customers with everything from financing and staff training to store design. VWR Corporation, a US$500 million distributor, sends its own staff to manage the storeroom of Chevron. They are also taking over purchasing for some DuPont research units. The Royal Bank of Canada finds that lending money is only one of the many services their customers need. Sixty per cent of their small business customers are non-borrowing. They want sound business advice and information. American Express will go into a business and offer to provide many of their internal reports, providing purchases are made with their credit cards.

Finding Your Niche

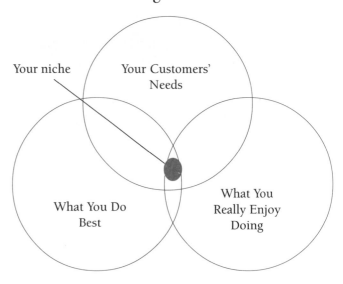

Your niche

Your Customers' Needs

What You Do Best

What You Really Enjoy Doing

What problems do your customers have running their businesses, satisfying their customers or doing business with you? Find them. These problems are your areas of opportunity where you can add value through increased benefits.

The Fifth Step

Talk To Your Customers' Customers

The best way to understand your customer's business is to talk to their customers — even if you are selling directly to the end-user. Each of us has customers to satisfy, be they purchasers, clients, friends or family members. If you can understand what your customers' customers need from them, you will see products and services that you could provide to help your customers succeed. Moreover, given your deep understanding of your business you will see opportunities that your customer would never see themselves. Business opportunities are lost when the customer does not know what the supplier can do and the supplier does not know what the customer really needs. Anything you can do to help your customers satisfy their customers they will value because the benefits will be obvious.

The best way to understand your customer's business is to talk to their customers.

Very few businesses do this well. Most, in fact, do only an average job of understanding their customers, never mind their customers' customers. When was the last time you sat down with your customer's customer?

You Want Partners

Having people who think of themselves as merely your customers is not enough for long-term and sustainable profitability because mere customers are too easily poached. If you are striving to be number one, you need customers who believe that you are so important to their own success that they cannot imagine being in business without you.

Partners are customers who believe that you are so important to their own success that they cannot imagine being in business without you.

Customers who see you as someone who could help them to succeed will want you as their partner. They will be keen to stay with you over the long term and will not desert you because your competitor offers them a 5 per cent discount or some other monthly special. They will buy from you because

Whether it's a bank or a car manufacturer, the institution that can identify its customers' needs and address them with prompt, expert advice will win its customers loyalty.

Canadian Banker,
January 1997

We try to build personal relationships with our suppliers — we expect good prices and good service and in return we're committed to them for a long time.

Fardad Moayeri,
an account executive with
Cold Private
Manufacturing Inc.

they know the lost opportunity cost of not buying your product or service is far greater than the cost of buying it. As we have seen, loyal customers are essential to your future success.

Partnering is rapidly replacing the traditional selling relationship. Smart business leaders do not concentrate on finding more effective ways to sell, they focus on developing compelling reasons for customers to buy. They know that many sales cannot be closed because the customer knows what you want him to do but not why he should do it.

Having partners rather than customers will become increasingly important over the next few years. As more and more companies practice the principles of quality management, they will be looking to have closer relationships with fewer preferred suppliers. Large corporations are even reducing the number of law firms they deal with. DuPont is aiming to cut its number of legal suppliers from 200–300 to between 30 and 50.

If you can give your customers more value than they can obtain either by themselves or from any other supplier, then you are prime partnership material. But developing a partnership is harder than it looks. It requires new attitudes and behaviours on both your part and that of your customers. The old view was that selling was about pushing the customer

We All Have Customers — Even Parents

Even the end-user or consumer has customers they are trying to please.

An ice cream shop in a shopping mall in Surfers Paradise, Australia, understands this. Like all ice cream parlours they keep their product in a display cabinet so people can see the flavours they have for sale.

What is unique about this store is that bolted on to the front of each display cabinet is a stainless steel ladder. Small children can climb up and see the tubs of ice cream.

This makes it easier for the parents to make their children, who are their customers, successful in obtaining the ice cream they want.

into making a purchase that enhanced your profitability. The aim of the partnership relationship must be for both parties to win. No longer can either party attempt to exploit the other by seeking out short-term advantages. You must follow the principle "If you win, then I win". Partnering requires an openness that, in turn, requires a high level of trust. You must be prepared to share your ideas, knowledge and limitations. Your customers, on the other hand, put all their eggs in one basket. In return for taking this risk, customers want to join with a reliable supplier of solutions who can help them be at the leading edge of their industry. You have to be proactive in determining their needs and be able to discover opportunities to add value they cannot see themselves. Most importantly, you have to be committed to looking after their wellbeing over the long haul.

Several companies have succeeded in building lasting and mutually beneficial partnerships. Many large retailers have electronic data transfer systems linking their stores to their suppliers. This allows the suppliers to know immediately about sales and stock movements so that they can do what is necessary to replenish the shelves. Proctor & Gamble works in partnership with the world's largest retailer, Wal-Mart, to keep them supplied with competitively priced products.

Four Steps For Turning Customers Into Partners

1. Identify key customers with whom you can develop a strategic partnership. Look for businesses which have problems you can solve in such a way as to give them a competitive advantage.

2. Get inside their business by working with their staff and talking to their customers to identify problems they have that you could solve.

3. Invest in developing the expertise and the technology to create systems which produce solutions to customers' problems.

4. Set up joint teams to review and improve both the solutions you provide and the systems that produce them.

You must be prepared to share your ideas, knowledge and limitations.

Scott Panel and Hardware, suppliers to the American joinery and furniture-making trade, has pledged to "forge a partnership with our customers". This includes not only supplying raw material but also practical help on business management. CEO Bob Linton quickly discovered there was a direct link between customers who were doing very well and his own profitability. As a result, Scott has appointed a business advice manager to coordinate a programme for their customers which includes running seminars on everything from the Fair Trading Act to cash-flow management. Linton's company is a showcase for his customers, who are encouraged to make site visits. If they see something they like, Linton's people will show them how to do it in their own companies.

In a similar vein, UPS has developed a partnership with one of its key customers, Motorola. UPS radically redesigned Motorola's distribution process and eliminated multiple handling. Delivery time was reduced by 75 per cent as a result. Products are now consolidated from Motorola's eight semiconductor plants in Asia and delivered by UPS directly to the customer's door in the USA. The next step is to turn ownership of the programme over to a UPS subsidiary which can provide Motorola with a broader array of services such as warehousing and inventory management.

Do your staff know how much new business comes from the companies each customer refers to you?

Advocates Are Even Better

If you work in partnership with your customers and make them successful you will be amply rewarded. In the automobile industry, suppliers with partnership arrangements with their customers are earning higher margins. But not only will partners repay you by buying more products and services at higher margins, they will tell others how great you are. This advocacy is the kind of advertising money cannot buy. And it is free!

Sheila Kessler, author of *Total Quality Service*, believes that each customer of Minute Maid orange juice provides US$26,000 by word of mouth advertising alone. This and other examples suggest businesses should strive for relationships with their customers where the customers are so excited about the products and services they are provided with that they want to tell others about their experience. You want your customers to be so enthusiastic about you that they will put their own reputations on the line to support you.

How many of your customers are actively referring business to you? That's a question that Irv Shapiro, CEO of Metamor Technologies, a US$7.9 million computer consulting company in Chicago, asked himself. He decided that the answer was not many, so he introduced an employee bonus scheme for staff whose clients agreed to be advocates for Metamor. Up to 10 per cent of the employee's salary is eligible to be paid out as a bonus. Each quarter, supervisors call customers and ask them if they are satisfied with the service, problem solving and communication from the consultant. If they are, the customers are asked if they will become advocates for Metamor. If they agree, the bonus is paid to the employee or team of employees handling the account. In 1994, over US$200,000 was paid out in bonuses. Shapiro does not mind, referrals from customers is way up.

It takes work to turn prospects into customers, and even more effort to turn customers into partners and then eventually advocates. But it is worth the time and energy because partners and advocates are your future security. They become something you have that your competitor cannot easily copy. They are assets you have built up.

The longer you work in partnership with your customers, the more they will become your advocates. And that has got to be good for your future growth.

Partners and advocates are your future security. They are assets you have built up and they cannot easily be copied by your competitors.

Summary

• **Neither customer service nor customer satisfaction are enough to succeed in this marketplace.** Studies show that the majority of customers who defect to another supplier were happy or very happy with the service they got from their original supplier. To be second to none, you must work to make your customers successful.

• **There are five steps to making your customers successful** beginning with the philosophy "If you win, I win". Everybody in your company needs to understand that this is the principle by which you wish to operate your business.

• **Choose the key customers you wish to target.** You do not have sufficient resources to treat all customers the same way. In this age of specialization and niches, you cannot be all things to all people.

• **Build a relationship with your customers.** Relationships take time and effort to build, but without them you have a lot of products and services to sell but few buyers.

• **Use this relationship to become part of their business.** The more you understand about your customer's business, the more opportunities you will see to make them successful.

• **One of the best things you can do is talk to your customer's customers.** That way you will see opportunities to help them that they cannot see.

• **The more you are part of your customers' success, the more they will want to work in partnership with you.** They will seek a long-term relationship and this is where your future success lies — in having loyal customers whose business you can retain.

• **The longer you work in partnership with your customers, the more they will become your advocates.** And that has got to be good for your future growth.

How Are *You* Doing?

How much of your time is spent doing things that do not create value for your customers?

And for each of your staff? Ask them!

Do you measure your customer defection rate?

If yes, what is it and how does it compare with that of your competitors?

What do you know about why some of your customers have defected?

What is the opportunity cost (lost future business) of losing these customers? What is the cost of recruiting replacement customers?

Which business in your town has the lowest defection rate? What are they doing differently?

How much time do you schedule to systematically work to build relationships with your key customers?

How would you rate you relationship-building skills? (circle one)   Poor   Average   Good

What are your strengths in this area?

And your weaknesses?

Give yourself a score of 1–5 on the following people skills, where 1 is poor and 5 is excellent.

• Listening

• Communicating your feelings

• Problem solving

• Managing conflict
(If you are male and you rated yourself a 5 on numbers 1, 2 and 4 get a second opinion.)

How much time do you spend maintaining your key relationships?

What do you do?

What are you doing right now to make your customers successful?

For each of your key customers, list the customers of theirs you have talked to.

What have you learned about what your customers' customers need from your customers to succeed?

What can you do to help your customers make their customers successful?

What opportunities are there for you to develop new business?

What are you doing to develop this business?

Which customers have you targeted to form strategic partnerships?

What problems do they have that you could help them to solve?

What are you doing to develop solutions to these problems?

Which joint teams could you set up to review and improve these solutions, and to find even more new business opportunities for your company?

✷ Strategy 5

Reduce The Costs

Reducing the costs your customers must pay is a very powerful way to increase value because consumers today are very cost sensitive. Price, however, is not the only cost to focus on. A competitive advantage can be gained by reducing the costs of ownership, effort, time and exposure to risk. Make your products and services inexpensive to use and your company easy to do business with. Focus on convenience for the customer and on doing things quickly. Review your business processes to ensure they are working efficiently. Most of all, be a reliable supplier and help your customers to trust you.

Lower Those Costs

The equation *value* = *benefits* – *costs* suggests that one of the most powerful ways to increase the value of your products and services is to decrease the costs your customers must pay. Research by such organisations as Environics Research Group in Canada shows that buying patterns are shifting towards spending less while finding increased benefits. This trend is attributed to an aging population which has less disposable income and is worried about unemployment and retirement. But even the wealthy are price sensitive. Forty per cent of American millionaires drive cars that are at least three years old.

If you aim to be second to none, you must reduce the costs your customers have to pay. I am not just talking about reducing your price because, as we discussed in Strategy 2, getting into a price war with your competitors will do no one any good in the long term. Certainly, you must be price competitive. Indeed, in most cases your price will need to be within 10–20 per cent of your major competitor's or customers are likely to reject you out of hand. But avoid competing on price

*Customers will be
afraid to make a
purchase if they do
not understand how
to use your product
or service, if they
see possible prob-
lems with it or if
they do not believe
what they heard
you say about it.*

*In return for their
patronage, con-
sumers want instant
service and
convenience around
the clock, access to
information and
protection against
invasion of their
privacy. They also
want the accuracy
and efficiency of
computers, and they
have little tolerance
for human error.*
Canadian Banker,
January 1997

alone. It will reduce your financial viability and may well threaten your entire industry.

A better strategy for increasing value is to reduce the other costs of acquiring the benefits from your products and services. In many markets, these costs are less affordable than the price and will prevent customers from buying. You will recall from Strategy 2 that, other than price, the main costs customers have to pay are:

1. The cost of ownership
2. Effort
3. Time
4. Exposure to risk

These costs are always in your customers' minds. The large North American retailer, Sears, surveyed 7000 of its customers about credit cards, and found that their customers wanted increased savings (reduce the price), convenience (reduce effort) and security (reduce their exposure to risk). A competitive advantage is to be gained by developing products and services, and also by improving ways of doing business, that reduces those costs.

The Cost Of Ownership

As anyone who has ever bought a car knows, there is the dollar cost of purchasing the vehicle and the dollar cost of owning it. High maintenance or operating costs, and the costs of insurance and parking, can all make the purchase price look cheap. It is the same with most products and services. To financially sensitive people — and who is not these days — you can increase the value of your offerings by reducing the costs of ownership. Although the costs of ownership will vary from one product and service to another, there are some common ones.

One of the first is the cost of installation. Large appliances and pieces of furniture have to be delivered, complicated bits of equipment like PCs have to be put together, and machinery has to be set up. In the past, these have typically attracted a cost which the customer has had to bear on top of the purchase price, but in a world of diminishing resources this is

No Free Lunches

There are no free lunches in this world. Every benefit has a cost. Price, however, is only one cost and often the easiest to pay.

1. Price	Compete on this and your product or service is likely to become just a commodity item.
2. Cost of ownership	These include the cost of installation, staff training, operation and maintenance and cost of replacement.
3. Effort	It takes effort to make money and effort to spend it.
4. Time	No one has enough. It is a big price for customers to pay.
5. Exposure to risk	Whenever you buy, there is risk. Will it work? Would I have got a better deal elsewhere? Will my supplier let me down?

often enough to stop potential customers from completing the purchase. The same applies to services. Customers have to be hooked up to pay TV or cable TV. It is interesting to see that in a number of countries suppliers of these services are waiving the installation charge in order to attract more customers. Most credit card companies used to charge an annual membership fee but the trend now is for companies to introduce new products that have no membership fee associated with them.

An increasing number of businesses are discovering that they can attract buyers by reducing, or even eliminating, the cost of obtaining a service or installing a product. Look at the world through your customer's eyes (Strategy 3) and identify the dollar costs they must pay to use your products and services. Remove these costs and see your business increase.

Another cost of ownership that hits the customer almost at the time of purchase is the cost of training staff to be able to use the product or service. More and more companies are bundling these costs with the purchase price and providing "free" on-site installation and staff training. Alternatively, by designing easy to use products and services, this cost can be avoided or, at least, significantly reduced.

It is a mistake to strip all of the costs out of the purchase price to be the lowest priced supplier and then hit customers with on-going service costs after the sale.

Further down the track, customers will encounter general operating costs such as energy and consumable materials, as well as on-going servicing and maintenance costs. The more you can eliminate or reduce these through improved designs of your products and services, the better. If you cannot, then look at taking over this work for your customer at no or low

Typical Costs Of Ownership

1. Installation cost.

2. Cost of training staff.

3. Operating costs.

4. Servicing and maintenance costs.

5. Compliance costs.

6. Upgrading and depreciation costs.

cost. In manufacturing, many suppliers monitor much of the equipment for their customers. Thus, a bearings company might do regular vibration analyses on pumps to see when the bearings need to be replaced. This saves both time and money for their customer.

Finally, where there is an on-going cost of use that the customer must pay, look at how you package it. Customers will perceive more value if you load these costs into the purchase price and then provide the services "free of charge". Many companies are so concerned about being the lowest priced supplier that they strip all of these costs from the purchase price and then present them to the customer one after another at a later date. This is a mistake. Although the customer might perceive they are getting a good deal at the time of purchase, as time goes on they will see only cost after cost and little additional benefit. They might also tell a lot of other people how they feel. For example, every month banks produce a statement showing customers:

- a fee for cashing each cheque deposited;
- a monthly activity fee;
- a monthly management fee;
- a monthly commitment fee;
- interest due on the overdraft.

These are five or more monthly reminders of the cost of using their services.

These statements provide no information about the benefits the bank has given the customer, they are just reminders of the cost. Law firms are also bad at this. They charge their clients hundreds or thousands of dollars for legal work and then add to the bill $15.96 for photocopying. Suppliers of products make this mistake, too. You can pay $40,000 for a new car and then be charged a relatively small sum for the 10,000 km service. And, banks, law firms and car dealers wonder why people hate doing business with them!

Yet another expensive cost of ownership can be compliance costs with government regulations, especially in the areas of health, safety and the environment. Apart from designing your products and services to make it easy to comply there is little that you as a supplier can do in this area, but you can make sure that your customers know what costs to expect. Your customers do not like surprises. They have learned that in business, 98 per cent of all surprises are bad.

> *Your customers do not like surprises. They have learned that in business, 98 per cent of all surprises are bad.*

Finally, there is a cost of ownership that occurs towards the end of the life of the product or service the customer has bought, and that is the cost of upgrading and the depreciation costs. Many people delay buying PCs because they believe that in a few months what they have bought will be out of date. What suppliers must get across is yes, there will be new models out but the one you are buying now will give you benefits for years. One of the challenges facing the car industry is that people are hanging on to their vehicles for five to seven years instead of trading them in two to three. Is it that people do not like new cars anymore? No, it is because they are not prepared to pay the depreciation cost in trading in. Cadillac maintained a competitive advantage over Lincoln for many years because their cars retained their value at trade in. Customers took this into account at the time of purchase.

Look at these and any other costs of ownership that are associated with your product or service. Try to eliminate them. If you cannot eliminate them, reduce them. When they are as low as they can go, package them in such a way that your customers see the benefits associated with those costs. Make sure that your customers know what costs are in store. You may make one sale by hiding them, but when your customers do discover them you will lose repeat business and maybe a number of potential customers will be put off by your ex-customers comments.

The Cost Of Effort

> *A nation full of people with little time is a market that competes on convenience.*

Dr M. Scott Peck got it right. The first three words of his bestseller, *The Road Less Travelled*, says it all: "Life is difficult."

We are all busier than we have ever been. Even people who are retired say they do not know how they ever found the time to work because being retired is a full-time job! Certainly in the workforce people are having to take on more work thanks to down-sizing. Most households are two-income families, houses seem to be bigger, requiring more looking after, and our children have a million extracurricular activities they have to be driven to and from. If you feel tired, you should. Research is beginning to confirm what we all feel: We are getting less sleep. A nation of working people with families and little time to spare is a market that competes on convenience.

Products and services that were easy to use have always sold better. When the band aid was first invented by Earl Dickson of Johnson & Johnson, it was made in strips 3 inches wide by 18 inches long. The user had to cut a strip to the right size to cover the wound. Sales were slow. Then Johnson & Johnson bought a machine that would cut the band aid into 3 inch by $3/4$ inch slices. Sales increased by 50 per cent in one year. Bay Milk in New Zealand developed a spreadable butter by mixing anhydrous milkfat with other ingredients. Because it is so easy to spread, the butter has became a huge success in Europe — so much so that countries like Britain found some non-tariff trade barriers to prevent its entry into their markets. The product is now manufactured in Europe using European milk.

In North America, 69 per cent of mothers with children under the age of 16 years work outside the home.

In the area of technology, most consumers believe that simplicity is good. Most consumers find their lives are complex enough without having to invest time taking a course in electronics in order to be able to use the home VCR. The product itself needs to be simple to use and any instruction manuals need to be easy to understand. Smart retailers of such goods install them for people, thus reducing one of the costs of ownership. In service areas, people want simplicity too. Corporate clients want their legal firms to keep it simple. "Give me something simple that works," I heard one senior manager say. "Don't try to impress me with a complex document or an elegant solution." No matter what your product or service, consumers want to be able to use it quickly and easily, without fuss or frustration. Time taken to master the use of a product or service will detract from its value in the eyes of the customer.

Business people who can develop products and services that allow their customers to succeed in the lifestyle they have chosen will do well. One example of such a company is a Danish supermarket chain, called Dansk, which approached

There are some very profitable niches and significant competitive advantages to be gained by arranging your business to fit in with your customer's lifestyle.

a New Zealand meat company looking for a supply of lamb to sell in the Danish market. They started out with traditional cuts such as frozen legs, but then the two firms worked together to produce 13 branded products which, for customer convenience and quick and easy preparation, were designed in set weight packs. The lines have been a roaring success and Dansk has captured 35 per cent of the market share for lamb in Denmark.

Business at the food drive-ins is booming because people want the convenience of rolling up to the window, getting their food and driving off to that next appointment. But eating lunch in the car can be a tricky business and showing up for that next sales presentation with ketchup on your best suit is no picnic. Thus, another opportunity for a product that allows us to live the lifestyle we choose. Pacific Sportswear of San Diego have solved that problem by developing the *twist away tray*. This re-usable tray hangs around your neck and pops open to protect your chest and lap from those embarrassing spills. When you are finished, you just wipe the tray clean, fold it back into its pouch and put it in the glove box.

There are examples of lifestyle products in the service industry, too. Some banks are trying to gain a competitive advantage by making it possible for people to bank from home via their telephone or computer. Canada Trust established an interactive voice-response system that allows customers to conduct from their homes virtually any business normally done at bank branches — such as bill payment, credit applications, cheque orders and payment tracing. Service is available seven days a week, 24 hours a day in English, French, Mandarin and Cantonese. Other banks and some credit card companies have developed products that will make it easier for people to track their money. Customers give them a code they would like to use to organize their expenses and the financial institutions sort their purchases by type and provide a breakdown for the customer's financial records.

More people eat out today than ever before. But people are also very health conscious so traditional fast foods are not what they seek. A whole industry is developing in selling *home*

In 1994, 50 per cent of all food consumed in the USA was cooked outside the home. It is expected to increase to 65 per cent in the near future.

replacement meals. These are healthy, home-style prepared meals that consumers would make for themselves if they had the time, the skill or the desire. Boston Market, founded in 1985 as Boston Chicken, is considered to be a pioneer in the home replacement meal market. There are now 1000 Boston Markets throughout the USA, with a new store opening every day. Boston Markets is very careful to maintain the homestyle image so no microwaves are used in food preparation.

Supermarkets which once thrived by providing only the ingredients for the meal must now go further if they wish to survive. Seven of every ten new supermarkets opening in the US have prepared food sections and four out of ten feature fast food style service with seating areas.

We don't want to replace Mom, but we want to replace her cooking.
Chris Dickinsen,
Regional Spokesperson
for Boston Markets in
Colorado

Many consumers are saying that not only are they too tired to cook but they are too tired to stop off and get take-away food. To make it even more convenient for people to eat tasty, healthy food, many restaurants are offering a home delivery service and some are even delivering to the office for those working longer hours.

Indeed, home delivery, which was common in the 1940s and 1950s before two-car families became the norm, is making a comeback. People want to shop in their homes and the direct selling business is expanding as a result. From 1991 to 1995 the Direct Selling Association charted a 38 per cent increase in the growth of direct retail sales and an increase of 41 per cent in the number of people involved in the industry. In almost every business sector from groceries to gifts you can find an entrepreneur who will take your order and deliver the product or service to your home. Call Doctor Inc. in San Diego, Doctors to Your Door in Kentucky and Health Drive in Massachusetts send doctors, dental and eye care specialists to homes, offices and nursing homes. SOS-Preservatifs will even deliver a condom to your home between the hours of 4 p.m. and 3 a.m. Now there is a business that is committed to making its customers successful!

Every time a consumer has to leave home to run an errand, a business opportunity is revealed.
Don Peppers and
Martha Rogers,
The One-to One Future

It takes work to make money and it takes work to spend it. You have to locate possible suppliers and do research to see who has the best deal. Then you have to make contact with them which, as we saw in Strategy 3, can take a lot of

What customers want — at least a good many of them — is not shopping that is enjoyable but shopping that is painless.

Peter Drucker

effort if they have an automated phone system. Then perhaps there are problems placing the order, obtaining the product or service you want, getting it delivered to the right place or even paying for it. But in this hectic and demanding world, effort is a big cost to pay.

It Takes Work

It takes work to make money and it takes work to spend it.

Add value to your products and services by making it easy for your customers to:

1. Find out about you

2. Visit your business

3. Make a choice

4. Make the purchase

5. Exchange it

6. Get after-sales service

Make It Easy

What your customers want is someone who is easy to deal with — someone who can add value through convenience. They want things to be easy and to be simple. Some businesses, like Wal-Mart, understand this. They know that busy customers want convenience — not sales clerks falling all over them. Customers would rather have well laid out and brightly lit stores that are full of a wide range of products which provide the best value in their category. They want the products in stock on the shelves and they want to get in and out fast.

The first step is to make it easy for people to find out about you. This is basic marketing but important nevertheless. People who do not know you exist are not likely to become your customers. Get name recognition by advertising, using signs, getting publicity in the local media and by networking. Also, make sure that key gate-keepers know who you are. For example, lawyers doing property conveyance would want to be known to real estate agents.

People who do not know you exist are not likely to become your customers.

But you need to go beyond name recognition. It is simply not enough for people to know who you are. They must also know *what* you are. What business are you in? What are your unique skills, products and services? What are the benefits you offer? And what costs must people pay? In other words, potential customers in your target market need to understand what value you can offer to them.

The next step is to make it easy for people to visit your place of business. Location, location, location is still critical. And it must be a convenient location that can be reached easily. Downtown core areas are in trouble because no one has time to go out shopping on their lunch hours any more (What's a lunch hour?) and because when they do drive into town there is difficulty with parking. Malls are closer to where people live and are surrounded by acres of free parking. Some malls even provide valet parking. At least that is what the fellow wearing the balaclava said he was doing!

It is simply not enough for people to know who you are. They must also know what you are.

Hurried and harried customers want the convenience that comes through one-stop shopping. Even in the commercial world, companies want to deal with suppliers who can look after a large number of their needs. In fact, most companies would rather have strategic partners than suppliers. A manufacturer does not want to buy packaging material from several different businesses. It would like to purchase cartons, plastic wrapping material and pallets from one company. If the truth were known, the manufacturer would probably like that supplier to set up shop in their factory, provide the packaging materials, actually do the wrapping and packing of their products and then arrange for them to be shipped to the customer. After all, the manufacturer does not want packing material, they want a solution.

Sound far-fetched? Volkswagen is doing that in their new US$250 million factory in Resende, a rural town in the state of Rio de Janeiro, Brazil. Seven main suppliers will make components for Volkswagens right in the plant using their own equipment. Then Volkswagen's workers will fasten the components together to make the finished trucks and buses. Why has Volkswagen organized its business this way? Because it is more convenient for them. Their suppliers are on-site and easily accessible. The components they are manufacturing are on hand and do not need to be shipped in. Quite simply, this arrangement makes it easier for Volkswagen to concentrate on their core business of building trucks and buses. Every company has its core competency — that thing it is really good at. Smart companies want to focus on their core business. Any supplier who makes it easy for them to do that, is going to be successful.

It is not just commercial customers who want one-stop shopping. Consumers in general would like all of their suppliers to be in one location. Suburban shopping malls do this to some extent, but the concept can be taken further to what Faith Popcorn, (yes, that really is her name) in her first book, *The Popcorn Report*, calls "cluster marketing". Cluster marketing, says Popcorn, would bring together a number of services and products into all-in-one centres. A kiosk in a downtown parking lot could become a depot where you post your letter, drop off your dry cleaning, buy the morning newspaper and arrange to have your car serviced. This is not an outlandish idea. As Popcorn points out, automated teller machines in

If a veterinarian and a taxidermist located their businesses on the same premises, what would their slogan be? "Either way you get your pet back."

many parts of America are already dispensing stamps, transit tickets and gift certificates.

In San Diego there is a combined self-service pet wash and espresso coffee bar called Poochies. For $7 you get all the things you need to wash your dog, use of an automated dog dryer (truly, I don't make this stuff up), tips on dog grooming and someone to clean up. You can also buy a cup of coffee to drink, something to eat and any number of pet-care products. What other products and services could you bundle with your existing offerings to make it easier for your customers to shop?

When customers think of visiting you, they do not necessarily intend to be there in person. In this electronic world, people are used to working anywhere so they want to be able to shop anywhere, too. You need to be connected. You need to be on-line. Many of your customers, and this number is increasing daily, want to be able to log in from anywhere in the world at anytime and be able to place orders, have payment approved and arrange delivery — all done 24 hours a day, seven days a week. The global marketplace never closes.

The next step in reducing the cost of effort is to make it easy for your customers to decide which product or service is best for them. This does not mean overwhelming them with choices, but rather removing the complexity from the buying decision. Identify what your target market is looking for, and either research the marketplace to see what is available that best matches their needs or produce a product or service that has the specifications they are looking for. It is easy to make the decision to buy when you are shown exactly what you want for the price you think is reasonable!

It is also easy to make a choice when dealing with staff who are competent: that is to say, when they have the product knowledge and the expertise required to be of assistance. In retailing today, it is common to talk to sales staff who have no idea about the features of the products they sell. This is particularly true in department stores selling high-tech products such as computers. It is a problem in the service industry, too. I once got into a taxi in a strange city and gave the taxi driver the address I wanted to go to. "Where's that?" he said helpfully. "How do I get there?" I got out and found another cab.

> *What other products and services could you bundle with your existing offerings to make it easier for your customers to shop?*

> *It is easy to make the decision to buy when you are shown exactly what you want for the price you think is reasonable!*

It is usually difficult and expensive to train staff with the necessary knowledge and skill, but some businesses turn this difficulty into a competitive advantage. I know of an outdoor recreation store that has sales staff who are themselves experts on wilderness and mountain survival. In an age where you are wise to occupy a niche, specialist knowledge is very important. But there is no point having this knowledge if it is not in the hands of the people who serve the customers.

Competent staff are not much good if they are not around. Customers want suppliers who are available when they want them to be, not when the supplier wants to be. A survey by Mastercard showed that 62 per cent of the customers interviewed said they had left a store without making a purchase because there was no sales clerk to help them. Some companies are using technology to remove the effort cost of hunting for a sales assistant by placing bar code scanners around the store which customers can use to find the price of an article. Canadian Tire have located service buzzers throughout their stores which customers can use to summon help. They also have touch-screen computers in their parts departments. These list all the auto parts they carry grouped by part type, then make, year and model of the car. When the customer finds the part they are looking for, they can print out a slip giving the name and description of the part, information about its use and where in the store it can be found, its price and its product number.

Yet another way to make it easier for customers to choose is to let them trial your product or service. I once read about a furniture store that let its customers trial furniture. Customers come into the store and select a few pieces which are then delivered to their home and later picked up, all at no cost to the customer. Similarly, I heard about a jewellery store that would mail a selection of watches to out of town customers who then made a choice and mailed the others back.

However you do it, it is in your best interest to make it extremely easy for your customer to choose a product and service to buy. It takes very little to deter some people from spending money, and for nearly everyone there comes a point when the level of doubt or confusion is sufficient to cause them to lose interest. If the decision becomes too hard and the customer loses interest, you lose a sale.

After making it easy for the customer to decide, you have to make it easy for them to buy. It sounds crazy, I know, but a lot of companies go to a considerable amount of trouble and expense attracting customers and then put barriers in the way when they try to order or pay for the product or service.

I once left a cellphone in a limousine in New York City. The limousine company found the phone and said they would send it to me in Canada providing I organized to have it shipped collect by one particular courier parcel company — and it had to be that particular company. (Have you ever tried to reason with a clerk in Queens?) I phoned the company and they said they would not take on the job unless the shipper had an account with them — even if it was being shipped collect. They told me that since the shipper did not have the required account (eventually we found out they did), I could not obtain the service I needed. No one at the company was prepared to look at any other options — including going to their local office and paying in advance. (Have you ever tried to reason with a clerk over an 0800 number?) Eventually I got through to a supervisor but she would do nothing. She would not even let me speak to a middle manager. All I kept hearing was the company policy. It was very frustrating. Eventually, after I behaved like the customer from hell, they found a way. But should you have to put that much effort into organizing what is essentially a very small and simple job? It took numerous phone calls and discussions to buy the service. It turned out to take over six weeks to get the phone moved 500 miles. And then they expected me to pay! Low benefits. High costs. Where is the value?

There is an increasing number of companies who recognize that making it convenient for people to buy is good for their business. Some design advertisements on television which emit an audible tone. If you hold the receiver of your phone up to the TV, the tone dials the company and you can place your order. Then there is a chain of Chinese restaurants in California called the Golden Wok. A customer can ring any outlet and the call is routed to the restaurant nearest their

> *If the decision becomes too hard and your customer loses interest, you lose a sale.*

house. A shopping mall in Canada puts out a list of gift ideas each Christmas. The list is sorted by age (child, teenager, grandparent) and gives a full description of the item, the store in which it can be found and the cost. A Gib board supplier in New Zealand will take your plans and arrange to place in each room of the building the precise quantity of Gib board in the right combination of sizes to do that particular room. A taxi company in the United States publishes a book of menus taken from local restaurants. Phone the cab company with your order and a uniformed driver will contact the restaurant to place the order and then pick it up and deliver it when it is ready.

The automobile industry is a very competitive one, and in the USA at least a number of companies are making convenience a competitive weapon. The trend in the used car business is to large chains of superstores. These are slightly more expensive, but customers do not seem to mind paying $500 for the variety, convenience and fast service. Customers go to a touch-sensitive computer screen and browse through 1000 or more cars. They choose a handful and print out the photos and features of the cars, and also where they are located on the lot. Without the computer, the choices would be overwhelming, but technology allows customers to hone in on a short list of cars that meet their needs without them having to pound the pavement.

Automatic Bills And Coins

More and more New York hotels are installing automated currency conversion machines in their lobbies. The machine in the Ramada Milford Plaza, a Broadway hotel where half the guests are foreigners, dispenses American bills and coins in exchange for Brazilian reals, British pounds, Canadian dollars, Dutch guilders, French francs, German marks, Israeli shekels, Italian lire, Japanese yen and Swiss francs.

The ten currencies accepted at the machine in the Novotel New York are the same as those at the Milford Plaza except that it does not take shekels or reals but does take Spanish pesetas and Swedish krona.

New York Times

"Woody" English, who owns a franchise of JD Byrider Systems in Avon, Indiana, also makes it easy for his customers to buy cars. Woody's business is to recondition and resell cars that are three to six years old. Every Byrider franchise owns a finance company which makes credit instantly available to purchasers. "It's a powerful sales weapon," says English.

Many other companies are also making good use of technology to make it easier for their customers to buy from them. Bill Tallent, for instance, runs a Sir Speedy franchise printing business in the USA. Tallent puts his own custom-made software into his customers' computers so when they have a job completed, the customer just double clicks on the company's icon on their computer screen and the job is automatically transmitted to Sir Speedy. It is then printed and the finished job is delivered to the customer. Tallent's competitive weapon is to link his technology with his business to save his customers money, time and effort.

Commercial customers are particularly interested in having suppliers who make it easy for them. To these customers, effort is money because they must hire people to do the work and in this age of downsizing, companies are looking to shed as much non-essential work as possible. Seeing this opportunity to provide extra value, many suppliers have taken over the responsibility for stock control. One of the most well known is the partnership I mentioned previously between Proctor & Gamble and Wal-Mart. P & G monitors holdings of products such as diapers and makes sure that minimum levels are met. New Zealand Sugar does this with many of its industrial customers by using telemetering to keep an eye on the level of sugar in their industrial customer's silos.

Customers want built-in flexibility. They want products that can be expanded, shrunk, upgraded and adapted to work with other systems.

Your customer is not interested just in products and services that are easy to use today, they also want something that has built-in flexibility so they can adapt it for use tomorrow. Thus, another aspect of convenience is flexibility. Customers do not want to be locked in. They want products and services that can be expanded, shrunk, upgraded and adapted to work with other systems. Modularize your products and services so people can mix and match. Make it easy for them to develop customized systems of their own by blending your products

How Could You Make It Easier?

A **florist** could offer to hold a list of special people and the dates (birthdays, anniversaries) customers wanted flowers sent. The flowers would be sent automatically with a handwritten note which the customer writes at the beginning of the year; the customer is billed afterwards.

A **gift shop** could do a similar thing but give customers a catalogue each year with a list of what was sent to whom in the previous years.

A **garage** could ring, tell you your car was ready for a service and then come and pick it up, leaving you a replacement car if necessary (or giving you taxi vouchers).

A **grocery store** could get a standing order of a customer's basic weekly needs and have these loaded into the shopping cart when the customer comes shopping. Then the customer simply looks for additional items.

A **pharmacy** could give you a quarterly record of drugs bought to make it easier to claim on insurance.

A **wine store** could let you know of new wines that have come in that they think, based on your usual buying patterns, you might be interested in. A **restaurant** could do the same thing with new dishes added to the menu or let you know when your favourite meals are on special.

A **photo store** could print the date, film number and negative number on the back of each photo.

and services with those from other suppliers. Computer software people, like Microsoft and IBM, should take note. The consumer wants plug and play. For most of us, our idea of an evening's entertainment is not interacting with the config.sys file!

In spite of your best efforts, things will go wrong. Your suppliers may let you down and give you faulty products. Your processes may fail and, as a result, you will not be able to deliver as promised. Or, perhaps your customer will just change their mind and want something different from what they bought. If these things happen, make it easy for your customers to return or exchange the product. Many businesses make the mistake of protecting themselves against the few customers who might cheat them by making their many *bona fide* customers jump through hoops to return a faulty product. Needless to say, this is not the way to increase customer retention. The more effort your customers have to spend getting a wrong righted, the greater the cost they have paid to deal with you. If you want to be second to none, your policy should be no questions asked, no receipt needed, immediate refund in full or exchange for another item of similar value. Make it easy for your customers to win, and you will win. Believe it. Live by it. Profit from it.

Finally, make it easy for your customers to get after-sales service. After-sales service enhances the value of your products and services because you make it easy for the customer to use them to their fullest capacity. In essence, you make it convenient for your customers to succeed. Many businesses are poor in this area. They are all over the customer like a rash when they want to make the sale, but do not seem to want to know them after the purchase has been made and the product taken home or the service used. Not only should you be very responsive to requests for after-sales service, but you should be proactive. Again, the more effort your customer has to put in to making your product or service do what they need it to do, the less value they will perceive and the less likely they will be to make repeat purchases. Set up systems to remind you to call your customers a few days after they have made the purchase and ask whether they would like any assistance. The very fact you cared to ring will make a big impression and probably motivate your customer to tell others about your service. Through one phone call you might turn an ordinary customer into a partner or even an advocate.

Your returns policy should be no questions asked, no receipt needed, immediate refund in full or exchange for another item of similar value.

Taking the effort out of using your product or service, doing business with you, or just plain living in this fast-paced and complex world can give you a tremendous competitive advantage. The easier you make it for people, the less cost they pay and the more value they gain. But telling your customers you will be convenient and doing it are two different things. To remove the effort for your customers you will need to operate effective and efficient work processes. You will especially need to shorten your cycle times. But mostly it will mean taking over more of your customers "work" and doing it for them while keeping the price the same or only marginally higher.

Be proactive in offering after-sales service. Through one phone call you might turn an ordinary customer into a partner or even an advocate.

The Cost Of Time

It certainly is a very fast-paced and busy world. All of us, especially working parents, find that more and more has to be crammed into the same old 24 hours. According to the *Yankelovich Monitor*, an annual report that tracks consumer values and lifestyles, 75 per cent of Americans believe their lives are too complicated. This is up from 50 per cent in 1985.

Work demands more of us. In the same Yankelovich poll, one-third of all Americans surveyed reported their jobs are more stressful today than a year ago. Certainly with downsizing we are working longer hours, and modern technology such as faxes and e-mail means that work can follow you home. Many people have their offices and businesses at home and find it very difficult to leave their work behind. They are constantly reminded of how much there is to do and how little time in which to do it. We are bombarded with more and more information that must be read and digested. Children today are just as busy, and since seven-year-olds cannot drive and public transportation systems leave a lot to be desired, that leaves Mum and Dad to don their chauffeur's cap. And there is still a lot to do around the house. Even if you got all of your meals prepared outside of the home, there is house cleaning and clothes washing. Apart from the microwave, there have not been any major time-saving appliances invented in the last 20 years.

Businesses are especially feeling the pressure of lack of time. Competition has increased and in this global economy their major threat could come from anywhere. Time must therefore be spent learning what is going on internationally and in developing strategic partnerships around the world. Customers have become more demanding and so have governments as regulations in the areas of health, safety and the environment make business more complex. Of course, most businesses have fewer people on deck.

Learn To Do Things Faster

To compete on value, you must learn to do things faster. Customers want to be able to contact you quickly. They do not want to have to sit and listen to canned music. They want to

> *People pay a big price when they have to invest time in buying your products and services. The faster you can do things, the more value you will add.*

> *People — individual consumers and buyers in general — just don't have time for poor service anymore.*
> Robert Tucker,
> *Win the Value Revolution*

be able to place an order in the shortest time possible. They do not want to waste their time giving you information that you already have on file from their last order but cannot retrieve. They want the product or service to be made and delivered to them fast. They are not prepared to wait while your inefficient processes ponderously grind out the work. Payment, say your customers, should be electronic. Customers can order over the telephone and have the product delivered by courier — probably by air. So, why should they have to post you a cheque? When things go wrong, they expect you to remedy it yesterday. Speed is so important to some customers that they are even willing to pay more if you can do things faster. Federal Express has built a very successful world-wide business on the backs of such customers.

Some companies are doing a very good job of doing things quickly. I was impressed when I went into a store in Canada and asked to join the *Air Miles* programme. Within minutes I had filled out the application form, been given an active card and was ready to start collecting the benefits. When I returned to New Zealand I went to join the *Fly Buys.* programme. I went to a local gas station where the attendant gave me an application form and told me to take it home, fill it in and post it off to head office. I would get my card, he said, in a week or two. How quaint!

When I went to stay at the Park Royal Hotel in Wellington, New Zealand, I asked to be picked up by their car. I was pleasantly surprised when, as we drove to the hotel from the airport, the driver checked me into the hotel and gave me my

Why Not, Indeed!

Edwin Land invented the polaroid instant camera because in 1943 his three-year-old daughter asked to see the pictures of her he had just taken.

Land explained that she would have to wait. It was not possible, he explained, to see the pictures until after they had got home.

"Why not?" asked his daughter.

"Why not, indeed," thought Land.

room key. Similarly, I appreciate the fast check-out facilities at many hotels around the world. It reduces the "cost" of staying at the hotel to have the bill slipped under the door on the last morning and to have to do nothing more than approve it and drop the key off as you walk out of the hotel.

Speed Matters

According to research done by the Centre for Customer-Driven quality at Purdue University, speed matters to your customers.

- 80 per cent of customers want the phone answered within four rings.

- 66 per cent will complain if they have to wait 30 seconds to talk to someone.

- 66 per cent want the first person they get to be able to handle the situation.

- 30 per cent think calls to an 0800 number should last no longer than 3 minutes — 49 per cent say 5 minutes or less.

- 70 per cent expect a reply to a letter within two weeks.

How fast are you doing these things?

Streamline Your Processes

Time is a major area of waste for everyone — not just customers. It is said that 25–40 per cent of the cost of producing a product and up to 50 per cent of the cost of delivering a service comes from waste. The biggest killer is wasted time, particularly in the service sector. Most of us do not know how much it costs to run our companies per person per minute, but if you worked it out you would get some idea of the cost of doing things slowly. Lack of speed can also be fatal to your business. Most small businesses fail because of lack of cash flow, not lack of orders. The faster you can get the order, fill it, ship it and send the invoice, the sooner you will get paid.

The secret to speed lies in your processes. You may be able respond quickly to any given situation by putting a bomb under yourself or your staff, but you will not be able to do it consistently. Your customers want you to do things fast not just when they make it urgent but all the time. To speed up your operation you must improve your business's processes.

Most large companies, and I suspect nearly all small companies, pay little attention to their business processes. They have exquisite organizational charts and, if they are quality-focused, they will have documented procedures. But few understand how the work really gets done — how it flows from person to person, team to team and department to department. One of the lessons businesses have learned from quality management is that after the customer, the process is the most important thing, because your business can never perform any better than your processes. If you wish to increase the value you offer your customers by reducing the time cost they pay, the best thing you can do is streamline your processes.

A process is a series of activities that takes an input and adds value to it to produce an output which is then passed on to a customer. The best people to streamline a business process are the people who are directly involved in the day to day operation of that process. Jobs are done by individuals, but because processes are a series of activities, they are operated by a team of people. The first step in streamlining your business processes then, is to organize your business into

Speed is really the driver that everyone is after. Faster products, faster product cycles to market and better response times to customers.

Jack Welch, CEO,
General Electric

How much does it cost you to run your business per person per minute?

After the customer, the process is the most important thing. Your business can perform no better than your processes do.

If you wish to increase the value you offer your customers by reducing the time cost they pay, the best thing you can do is streamline your processes.

What paper are you shuffling you do not even need? What time do you waste collecting information you already have? What information do you collect that you do not need?

teams of employees with each team being responsible for the operation of a process or sub-process.

Streamlined and efficient processes have as few steps as possible and are free of bottlenecks. I have spent many years helping companies to improve their business processes but every time I see a flow chart I am amazed at how convoluted most processes are. Unless you take the time to sit down and flow chart the entire process, no one knows the big picture. Each person sees their own little bit and although everybody knows that things do not happen as smoothly as they could, they do not understand why. It is most illuminating for a work team to come together and identify what actually happens as the work flows through the business. The resulting flow chart is usually full of opportunities to delete unnecessary steps, eliminate duplicated activities and to simplify operations. The result will be time saved for both your company and your customer.

Business processes can be streamlined by simplifying the paperwork. Most companies collect information they no longer need. They also collect information from their customers they already have somewhere else in their systems but have not figured out how to retrieve. These and other paperwork problems often exist because the company has progressed from manual systems to electronic ones, but is simply doing electronically what they always did manually. What paper are you shuffling you do not even need? What time do you waste collecting information you already have? What information do you collect that you do not need?

Another step to streamline your processes is to remove unnecessary control points, such as having things approved by a superior. Most companies have far too many control points built into their operation because they are afraid that front-line staff might not do the right thing or make the right decision. And they have good reason to be worried. If processes are not clear and procedures not documented then people will probably get it wrong. For example, if you did not know how to change the oil in your car's engine then you would have to be directed every step of the way. But if the process was clearly outlined in a manual you could be left to get on

Seven Steps To Streamline Your Processes

1. Organize your people into teams around their business processes.

2. Have each team flow-chart its business process.

3. Ask each team to streamline its process by:
- removing unnecessary steps;
- unclogging bottlenecks;
- simplifying the paperwork;
- removing needless control points;
- rescheduling some activities to avoid peak hour rushes;
- identifying activities duplicated elsewhere.

4. Ask each team to error-proof its process by
- finding commonly occurring mistakes
- identifying mistakes waiting to happen
- developing procedures to reduce the chances both of these could happen

5. Have each team measure how well its process operates.
- How long does it take to complete the process?
- Where do the delays occur?
- Where do things go wrong?

6. Have your teams review the performance of their process regularly.

7. Give the team the time and skills to improve its process.

with it. Needless control points cause delays as staff wait for someone with the required authority to give their approval. Empower your staff. Give them both the responsibility and the authority needed to create value for your customers.

Yet another way to streamline your business processes is to look at when the activities are performed. I have seen a number of situations where a key activity is undertaken at a peak time, causing delays for the customer. Rescheduling could make things happen faster. I once had an unscheduled stop-over in Hawaii due to mechanical problems with an aircraft. (It is a tough life but someone has to do it!) It was after 1 a.m. when two bus loads of tired passengers arrived to check into the hotel. Even though all costs were being paid by the airline company, everyone had to go through the complete check-in

Empower your staff. Give them both the responsibility and the authority needed to create value for your customers.

procedure, which included the time-consuming process of filling out the usual forms. This delayed the process so that it took nearly two hours to get everyone into their rooms. Why was this necessary? Surely taking people's names would have been enough since the airline was paying and knew who the passengers were. If the hotel wanted this information for their records they could have taken a name, handed out a key and asked the tried and frustrated traveller to come down next morning and complete a form. It would have made life easier for the hotel staff, too. They were looking pretty hassled. Rescheduling activities or reordering the process can save everyone a lot of time.

Error-Proof Your Processes

A major cause of delays is mistakes. When things go wrong rework is required costing you money and your customer time.

A major cause of delays is mistakes. When things go wrong and when mistakes are made, more work is required. That costs you money and the customer time. Waiting to get the product or service you ordered because someone goofed adds insult to injury. In such cases, customers are often told:

- *Mistakes do happen.*

- *Humans make mistakes.*

Now how would you feel hearing those words just before you got on an airplane?

Most people do not worry about flying because they know that air travel has one of the best safety records of any industry. How can this be when the planes are built, maintained and operated by human beings — the same animal species that makes mistakes in all other areas? Because in the world of air travel, processes, systems and procedures have been error-proofed. This means that knowledgeable people reviewed all processes in order to identify mistakes that did or could occur, and then took steps to make it unlikely these will happen. For example, a pilot might attempt to land the plane with the wheels up — an action that would be a cause of major customer dissatisfaction. Installing an alarm that sounds when the wheels are still up but the plane has descended to a certain level would make it unlikely the pilot would try to land in these conditions. This is what you should do. Bring your work teams together to review your current business processes and error-proof them. When things do go wrong, investigate the incident. Then, once you have found the root cause, take steps to prevent similar mistakes from occurring again. Remember, you are looking for the problem within the process, not for a scapegoat. It is better business to fix the problem than to fix the blame.

Reviewing business processes is not something that should occur only once. It should be an on-going activity. Give your work teams the time and the skills necessary to be able to measure the performance of their processes. They should pay particular attention to the cycle time — the time taken to complete the process from start to finish.

Give your work teams the time and the skills necessary to measure and improve the performance of their processes.

Reviewing, streamlining and error-proofing your business processes requires a commitment and an investment from you but it will be worth it. Do not underestimate how much time can be saved. It is not unusual to read about companies who, as a result of business process re-engineering, process improvement and the use of modern technology, do in weeks what previously took months, in days what took weeks and in hours what took days. When you look at the cost of making your processes more efficient, look at the cost of not doing it. You probably cannot afford the price that mistakes, delays and rework are costing you. Your customers certainly cannot afford the time inefficient processes cost them.

The Cost Of Exposure To Risk

One of the biggest costs customers pay is being exposed to risk. The risk may be very minor, such as being in trouble for having spent too much money or discovering the following morning that another shop has the identical item for 10 per cent less. At the other end of the spectrum, you might be exposed to the risk of losing a major customer because your supplier has let you down. Customers know that whenever they purchase from you there is some risk that they will lose something. The prospect of loss produces unpleasant feelings which usually take the form of frustration, anger, fear and humiliation. The bigger the loss your customers potentially face, the greater their anxiety.

Your customers cannot afford the time inefficient processes cost them.

The emotional cost customers pay due to this exposure to risk is the easiest and cheapest cost to reduce. Moreover, in a world where customer service and reliability are patchy at best, reducing your customer's exposure to risk can be a very powerful way to become number one in your market.

Reliability Matters Most

The biggest risk customers face is that something will go wrong — they will have purchased the wrong product, the service will fail, the goods will be delivered late. Most business leaders believe that price is the biggest factor affecting the customer's decision to buy, but this is not true. It is reliability.

No one wants to pay for something that does not work — even if the price is right! This is particularly true if your customers are in business themselves. Your commercial customers use your products and services to make what they sell to their clients. Over the years I have heard many of my own customers' customers say to them: "Yes, price is important but not nearly as important as reliability. It is worth a little more to us to deal with a supplier who will not let us down. The cost of a supplier's failure is very high."

Your performance scares your business customers to death because they are only too aware that you can put them out of business. The consequences of your poor performance are potentially so great for your customers they are not prepared to take it on faith that you can deliver what you promise. This is why so many companies insist that their suppliers have a quality assurance system in place to the level of an internationally recognized standard such as the ISO 9000 series. They want evidence that you, as their supplier, have the systems and processes in place to allow them to satisfy their customers. They are looking for *trustmarks*, not trademarks.

Customers Want To Trust You

Customers do not want to pay the emotional cost associated with exposure to risk. They get enough anxiety, worry and stress elsewhere in their lives. Customers want be able to trust their supplier. Trust, as we saw in Strategy 4 (page 109), is a feeling of confidence you have in someone when they con-

Like Ripples In A Pond

The effects of your poor performance can have widespread implications on the lives of other people, just like the ripples when a stone is cast into a pond.

My wife and sons were on a flight from Toronto to Honolulu with a connecting flight to New Zealand. A few minutes before departure, when everyone was sitting on the plane waiting for it to depart, the pilot announced that the company which refuelled the plane was having a problem. It seems that an employee had phoned in sick that morning and since they had no replacement worker everything was running a little behind schedule. In fact, the truck had only just arrived at the plane, the pilot told the passengers. He expected they would be refuelled quickly.

It took an hour to fuel up and by the time they took off, the plane was an hour and a half late. Approximately 270 passengers and crew were delayed 90 minutes because one man failed to show up for work. And this does not include any ground staff who might have been affected.

But the story does not end there. The plane was scheduled to connect with two other planes in Honolulu — one bound for Auckland, New Zealand and one for Sydney, Australia. Needless to say, the connecting passengers, who comprised probably two-thirds of those on the plane, were worried about missing their connecting flights.

"Passengers going on to New Zealand and Australia," announced the pilot en route to Hawaii, "don't need to worry about making your connections. We have arranged for those planes to be held until we arrive."

That was great news but it meant that another four or five hundred people were inconvenienced in Hawaii and it probably also affected ground staff, air traffic controllers and customs officials in Auckland and Sydney.

All told, between 800 and 1000 people were affected because one man failed to show for work and the company had no back-up plan.

sistently meet your expectations, and is the result of people doing what they say they are going to do. Trust is becoming increasingly important to customers. The Nineties has become a decade of doubt and cynicism. Research shows that 60 per cent of Americans are core distrusters, agreeing with the statement "Most people cannot be trusted", according to Eric Uslaner, a professor at Maryland University.

Developing this trust is not difficult because your customers would really prefer to trust you. They would much rather have feelings of confidence and security than anxiety and vulnerability. They just need some sign that you are trustworthy.

Customers do not want to pay the emotional cost associated with exposure to risk. They are looking for **trustmarks,** *not* **trademarks.**

Specifically, customers need three things if they are going to trust you:

1. To encounter friendly staff
2. Information
3. A performance guarantee

The first step to helping customers trust you is to provide friendly staff. This may seem like a small thing to you but it is important to your customers. We like friendly people and it is easier to trust people we like. We believe that friendly people have our best interests at heart and it is easier to trust people who care about you. Through customer surveys, British Airways learned in 1983 that having congenial staff was twice as important to customers as high quality food or pleasant airport lounges. Dealing with friendly people is quite soothing and that is a good antidote to anxiety. It is also very uplifting and therein lies another benefit of having congenial staff. Positive, enthusiastic and welcoming staff reduce the effort cost of doing business because the energy they give out more than replaces the energy taken to make the purchase.

Customers want to deal with staff who appear to care about them and who see them as being more than just another transaction. We have all seen The Phantom, the employee who is not really there. Like the fellow who served me in a grocery store and said not one word to me during the entire checkout procedure.

Or Oscar the Grouch. I met him one day at a gas station. I had just filled up with gas and went in to pay. As I walked up to the counter, the attendant called out: "Twenty dollars on the silver one, eh?" Thinking he was talking to me, I replied: "No, I just got fifteen dollars of bronze." Angrily, he shot back: "I was talking to the other guy, OK?" Sure, that is OK with me. I will just go somewhere else next time.

Then there is The Robot, the employee with the personality of an artichoke, who loves their job as much as you love a tax audit.

"Hi there. How are you today? I'm here to see Don Brown. I have a ten-thirty appointment."

"Name?"

"I'm Bob Johnson."

"Who do you want to see?"

"Don Brown. I have a ten-thirty appointment."

"Is he expecting you?"

"I think so. I have a ten-thirty appointment."

"Sit down. I'll tell him you're here. What did you say your name was?"

No matter which country I am in, I am struck by the huge variation in the friendliness of front-line staff. Some are very bubbly, out-going and personable while others are shy, indifferent or even surly. In fact, the variation rather reflects the range one encounters in the community at large, suggesting that business leaders pay little attention to this aspect of customer service. Perhaps managers forget that products and services are exchanged face to face. The commercial transaction is, from the customer's point of view, a social experience.

Hire for attitude.
Train for skill.
Herb Kellagher, CEO,
Southwest Airlines

Three Steps To Helping Customers Trust You

1. Provide friendly staff

We like friendly people and it is easier to trust people we like. We believe that friendly people have our best interests at heart and it is easier to trust people who care about you.

Hire people who have a positive attitude, friendly nature and who are enthusiastic about serving customers. Train them properly and give them support when they are on the job. Then reward them for good service. Remember, your staff will treat their customers the way you treat them.

2. Provide adequate information

Customers come to businesses not so much because of what they sell but because of what they know. They want information that helps them to make the right decision about the products and services they should purchase. They want to know how things are progressing. And they would like to know how the supplier has performed overall.

3. Offer performance guarantees

Performance guarantees significantly reduce the amount of risk the customer has to take because they reduce the cost the customer will have to pay if things go wrong. They also demonstrate the confidence you have in the value you offer. The money-back guarantee is very powerful. So powerful, in fact that I recommend you always give a full, no questions asked, money-back guarantee.

Hire people who have a positive attitude, friendly nature and who are enthusiastic about serving your customers. Such as the young man who served me in a shop in Honolulu. I asked him where I could find a certain item and he directed me to the right department. Later I saw him in a different store where he was shopping. He recognized me, came over and asked me if I had been able to get what I was looking for. That is the type of person to hire. Then train them properly and give them support when they are on the job. Finally, reward them for good performance. Remember, your staff will treat their customers the way you treat them.

The next thing that helps your customers to trust you is to provide them with adequate information. Many business people forget that customers come to them not so much because of what they sell but because of what they know. Customers want information that helps them to make the right decision about the products and services they should purchase and it is very annoying to them when they do not get it. I once went into a tourist information centre in a large city in the South Island of New Zealand. I asked the person behind the counter three basic questions and she could not answer one of them. She did not even have a map of the city to hand out. On another occasion my family and I were getting some fast food at a coffee bar in a tourist town in northern Ontario in Canada. I asked the young person who was serving us the price of the small, medium and large sizes of the drinks. She said she did not know and then she stood there looking at me. I finally suggested she go and find out. Even if people do have a reason for not knowing — because they are new to the business, the prices have changed or whatever — it does not help the customer. Customers want answers not problems.

Home Depot is one company that understands this. They have invested in staff who are knowledgeable and skilled in home renovations and they have told staff their job is to share that expertise with their customers. Home Depot has turned information into a competitive advantage as a result. Another company who has turned information into dollars is Coffee Beanery Ltd in Michigan (USA). This coffee chain found out from focus groups that their customers wanted more information about taste. As a result, the chain added product descriptions, samples and franchisee training about coffee. Was it worth it? In one month alone, same store sales increased 7.5 per cent over the previous year.

Customers would also like to know how things are progressing while the product is being manufactured or shipped, or while the service is being delivered. The longer the lead time, the greater the urgency, or the more the customer has to lose, the greater the customer's anxiety is likely to be and, therefore, the greater the need for progress reports. I once left some very expensive equipment behind in a hotel after addressing a conference. What was worse, I needed it in another city the next afternoon. I phoned the hotel from my car as soon as I had realized I had left without it. They promised to find my case and send it on to me. I was very impressed with the way the hotel phoned me back several times. The first call was to tell me they had found it. The second that arrangements had been made with a courier and the third call told me it had been picked up and was on its way. Compare that with an experience a friend of mine had with a courier in Canada. He arranged to have a parcel picked up and sent to his office express. It never showed up. Three days after it was due to arrive, he telephoned the shipper to find that it had never been picked up. My friend was annoyed that the parcel had not been collected but he was furious that no one had called to let him know. From the customer's point of view, no news is not good news.

The third step in promoting trust is to offer performance guarantees. This is a very powerful action because it significantly reduces the amount of risk the customer has to take. In many cases, if a full money-back, no-questions-asked guarantee is available, the worst-case scenario for the customer is likely to be the time and effort invested. In situations where poor performance on the part of a supplier could leave the customer in a precarious position with their customers, the cost could be much higher of course. Nevertheless, it is reassuring to a customer to see that its supplier is so sure about the value it can offer that it will risk working for nothing.

Money-back guarantees reduce the exposure to risk so

> *Customers come to you not so much because of what you sell but because of what you know.*

> *From the customer's point of view, no news is not good news.*

much that they make it very easy for people to buy. For example, a friend of mine wanted to buy something to put on his hair to stop it from drying out but since he had not used any such hair care products since Brylcreme went out of fashion, he was apprehensive to say the least. He explained his problem to a sales person in a hair care shop. The sales person quickly understood my friend's problem and straight away produced a product that he recommended. As my friend stood there hesitating and examining the bottle, clearly undecided, the sales person said: "Take it home and try it. If you are not satisfied with the results, bring it back within seven days and I will give you something else to try. If we don't find anything that works for you, I'll give you back your money." My friend was sold. What had he got to lose? The cost of exposure to risk had been reduced to next to nothing.

Money-back guarantees reduce the exposure to risk so much that they make it very easy for people to buy.

Mercury Energy, a power company in New Zealand, also offers performance guarantees. They promise to pay customers $20 if staff show up 15 minutes late for an appointment or if they can not restore power within four hours of it being cut off whatever the reason for the disruption in service. I was once at a meeting with Wayne Gilbert, the CEO of Mercury Energy, and someone asked him why his company would offer such an unconditional guarantee when the cause of the disruption in service could have nothing to do with them. For example, a drunk driver could hit a power pole, knocking down the lines and severing the power supply to a large number of homes. Why would Mercury Energy, the fellow asked, put itself in a position of having to pay a guarantee for situations like that? The CEO's response showed a good understanding of value.

"Power disruptions are a serious matter to our customers. They rely on us to give them an uninterrupted supply of electricity. That's what we get paid to do. If there is a disruption, our customers don't care why. They don't worry about what may have caused it. All they know is that they are not getting what they paid for.

"If we pay out enough money, maybe we will take the matter seriously, too. Maybe we will invest some time and money making it impossible for drunk drivers to stop our customers

Make It Safe To Buy

Take away the customer's risk of buying from you. Give free samples so that people can experience your product or service. Give free products and demonstrations. Give free consultations and free seminars. These soft steps let your prospective customers know what it is actually like to own what you are selling without taking any risks whatsoever. It gives them a chance to get to know you, to build a relationship and to learn to trust you.

from getting electricity. Maybe we will find ways to make these events things we can control."

Not every company has this commitment to delivering value. A major bank in Canada offered $5 if they kept customers waiting more than five minutes to see a teller. As the bank started cutting back on their staff numbers, I noticed the guarantee had been "refined" to use the words of the bank's senior vice-president. It no longer applied to people waiting to do transactions that could have been made through an automatic banking machine. The bank also admits it has forked out "over millions of dollars" in performance guarantees. Is the bank guilty of taking the easy way out? Has it decided it is easier to withdraw the guarantee instead of fixing the problems? Of course not. According to the same vice-president, the modification is just "educational awareness training for our customers."

Whereas many companies are just too quick to shrug their shoulders and say sorry when they or their products do not perform, guarantees like that from Mercury Energy suggest the company takes seriously its promise to do what it says it will do. Such guarantees usually inspire confidence in the consumer and stimulate sales as a result. Thirty-year-old Chris Zane is the largest independent bicycle dealer in New Haven, Connecticut. His business is growing 25 per cent each year. When the usual service guarantee on bicycles was 30 days, Zane offered a year. When competitors matched him, he extended it to five years. Today, he offers a 90-day price guarantee (find a lower price and we will match it) and a lifetime service guarantee.

It isn't that we build such bad cars, it's that they are such lousy customers.
Charles Kettering, President and Chairman of the Board of General Motors 1925–1949

> *The money-back guarantee is very powerful. Always give a full, no questions asked, money-back guarantee to show you have confidence in your product or service.*

The money-back guarantee is very powerful. So powerful, in fact, that I recommend you use it every time. Always give a full, no questions asked, money-back guarantee. Make the time limit long. Show people you have confidence in your products and services. And when the guarantee is asked for, honour it with a smile.

The Customer's Bill of Rights

The Quill Corporation, America's largest independent office products mail order dealer, sends out a one-page Customer Bill of Rights to its 500,000 customers. These rights include:

• full value for their money;
• guaranteed satisfaction;
• fast delivery;
• pre-authorized returns.

Do your customers have rights? Do they know them?

Be fast, convenient and reliable, and you will have reduced some of the most expensive costs customers have to pay. The next step to becoming second to none is to increase the benefits you offer, and the best way to do that is to give them something extra.

Summary

- **Do not compete on price alone**: **reduce the other costs** your customers have to pay. For many, these costs are less affordable than the cost of purchase.

- **The cost of ownership can be expensive** for customers. This cost comes from installing the product or service, the cost of staff training, on-going operating and maintenance costs, the costs of complying with government regulations and up-grading and depreciation costs. Any steps you can take to reduce these, either through better product and service design or through the way you operate your business, will add value in the eyes of your customer.

- **In this busy world customers are concerned with the cost of effort.** The more convenient you can make it for people to do business with you, the better. Make it easier for them to find out about you, to visit your place of business, to decide which product or service they want, to buy it, to get after-sales service and, if things go wrong, to exchange it or get a refund.

- **Customers are also concerned about the cost of time.** The faster you can do things, the better. Time can be a killer for you, too. Wasted time is costing you money and slow processes cause cash-flow problems. You can improve the speed of your operation by streamlining your business processes. Remove unnecessary steps and unclog bottlenecks. Simplify the paperwork and remove needless control points. Reschedule activities that clash with busy periods and identify activities duplicated elsewhere. Mistakes cause delays so error-proof your processes. Then measure the performance of your processes, constantly seeking ways to improve them — particularly to make them faster.

- **Finally, there is the cost of exposure to risk.** This is one of the biggest costs customers pay because exposure to risk causes your customers to feel anxious. This is a reality-based fear as your poor performance could put your customers out of business. You can minimize this cost by helping customers to trust you. Provide friendly staff, adequate information and offer performance guarantees.

- **Reducing these costs can give you a competitive advantage.** Customers cannot afford to pay them and will be attracted to a supplier who reduces them. It will also be difficult for your competitors to match you. Often customers will pay a financial premium to have these costs reduced.

How Are *You* Doing?

Which of the following costs of ownership is
most expensive for your customers:

- Installation cost?
- Cost of staff training?
- Operating cost?
- Service and maintenance costs?
- Compliance costs?
- Upgrading and depreciation costs?

What could you do to reduce these costs?

How easy is it for your customers to:

- Find out about you?
- Make a choice?
- Make the purchase?
- Exchange it?
- Get after-sales service?

Improving which one of these would give you a competitive
advantage?

What are your main business processes?

Which of these have been flow-charted or documented?

Which have been streamlined?

Which have been error-proofed?

Where is the greatest need for improvement? Look at customer complaints, slow performance and areas where work has to be redone

What is your customer's biggest exposure to risk? Where have you let them down?

How has this affected their business performance?

What has this failure cost your customers?

How well do you help your customers to trust you?

Do you have friendly staff?

Do you provide adequate information?

Do you give performance guarantees?

How quickly can you:

- answer the telephone?
- answer the customer's question?
- take the order?
- get the raw materials?
- make or source the product?
- deliver the service?
- approve credit?
- ship it to the customer?
- send out the invoice?
- arrange for payment?
- deliver after-sales service?
- exchange the goods?

How quickly could you do these things if you really had to?

What would you have to do to be able to do it that fast all the time?

 **Strategy 6**

Give Them Something Extra

To become second to none in this challenging marketplace you must give your customers more benefits. Some benefits are seen by the consumer as being simply hygiene factors. Do them well and nobody notices but do them poorly and you lose business. Other benefits are "delighters". They really excite and impress your customers.

There are three levels of creating benefits. The first two, creating benefits through your basic product and service, and creating benefits through providing support services, are hygiene factors. To delight your customers, you must give them something extra. Find those problems they would love you to solve but do not really think you could. Then solve them — at no extra cost. It sounds difficult, but many people have developed very successful businesses this way.

Your Aim: More Benefits For Less Cost

Those who succeed in this global marketplace will be those who give their customers more benefits for less cost. As we have seen, your price must be within range of the lowest priced supplier. You must also reduce the costs of ownership, time, effort and exposure to risk, but most importantly, you must increase the benefits you offer. And the best way to do that is to give your customers something extra.

There is no getting away from it. A lot of companies out there are trying to steal your customer's business, and with your customers having so many choices you must constantly strive to delight them. Things that satisfy your customers are just *hygiene factors*. Customers expect them and you will not get much credit for doing them well. But you will lose business if you fail to satisfy. Making products and delivering services that work; shipping goods on time to the right place without damage; having items in stock; being open all hours — these are things customers expect.

Hygiene factors do not impress any longer. *Delighters*, on the other hand, are things you do that customers do not expect. They are *something extra* and they take the customer by surprise. They can give you a unique competitive advantage as a result. Many companies, of course, talk about delighting their customers, but what many fail to understand is that delighters do not work unless the hygiene factors are in place. Customers would not be impressed, for example, with a restaurant that provided free valet parking and complimentary champagne but had slow service and cold food.

Delighters are something extra and they take the customer by surprise. They give you a unique competitive advantage as a result.

Level One

The Basic Product Or Service

The key to being able to delight your customers by giving them something extra is to understand that benefits are created at three levels. These are a hierarchy, so benefits must be being created at the previous level before the next can have any impact. As shown on page 172, the first level is to create benefits through your basic product or service.

Customers expect you to get the basics right because, first and foremost, they want a product or service that works. If you produce defective products and services, you will not make your customers successful (Strategy 3) and you will increase the cost of exposure to risk (Strategy 5), as the Kapiti District Council in New Zealand did when a group of mourners showed up for a funeral and found the grave had not been dug. Or as New Zealand Rail did when a square box car smashed into the sides of the Manawatu Gorge Tunnel. The tunnel is designed only for cars with rounded edges. And then there was the case of the exterminators who used a fumigation bomb that was so powerful that it blew the customer's house to bits.

Benefits are created at three levels. These are a hierarchy so that benefits must be being created at the previous level before the next can have any impact.

Getting the basics right is critical to both you and your customer, and is an essential part of creating value. A Canadian chain of ice cream parlours, called Cows, understands this. Every ice cream cone is weighed to make sure it meets the

Hygiene Factors	Examples Of Delighters
Products and services that work	A deli puts a little extra — a piece of fruit — in each lunch
Competent and friendly staff	Enthusiastic staff with expertise
Convenient location and hours	The store comes to your home
Good selection	An Internet connection gives a world-wide selection
Delivery on time and in full	A furniture company puts flowers in the middle of the dining room table it delivers
Market price	Market price with coupons to upgrade or add on
Performance guarantee	Life-time guarantee
Available if dissatisfied	Call to ask about satisfaction

standard of four ounces. At Cows you know you are getting what you paid for. Furthermore, no one ever believed they got value for money when they bought junk, no matter how cheap the price. Remember the Japanese products of the 1950s and early 1960s?

To become a reliable supplier of products and services that work you need to have your business processes working effectively. It is understood by managers today that the root cause in the vast majority of cases where things go wrong is a defect in the process not human error. In Chapter Three of *The Yellow Brick Road*, I used the tea-making process as an example of how blaming staff will accomplish nothing if the problem is a fundamental flaw in the process. You are better off to fix the problem, not the blame. This means bringing front-line workers together to review the process to find the fault and then to take steps to correct it. As we saw with Strategy 5, if you want to do things faster you must understand, measure and improve your business processes. The same is true for being reliable.

No one ever believed they got value for money when they bought junk, no matter how cheap the price.

171

The aim is to have a collection of "mini-businesses" within the larger business with each team being responsible for the success of its business.

If you have not already done so to speed up your business operation, the first step to making your business processes more effective is to organize your people into teams around their processes. The aim is to have a collection of "mini-businesses" within the larger business, with each mini-business being a team of seven to eleven people who are responsible for operating one business process or sub-process. The next step is to ask each team to flow-chart its process. This in itself will be a most illuminating activity. Each person on the team will learn a great deal about how the work actually gets done and when the flow-chart is finished the team will see a number of opportunities for improvement.

The third step is to ask each team to error-proof its process by having them identify mistakes that are happening now or that could happen. For example, a medium-sized shirt could be hung on the rack on a coat hanger marked XL, or a professional person could forget an appointment with a client. The team should then change the process so that it would be unlikely these mistakes would occur (see page 154).

Three Levels Of Benefits

Level Three: Delighters
Give your customers something extra.
Provide solutions to problems your
customers would love you to solve but
do not realistically expect you can.

Level Two: Support Services
These, too, are hygiene factors. They are
additional services that make it easier for
customers to benefit from your core product
or service.

Level One: Basic Product or Service
These are hygiene factors.
Get the basics right • Be a reliable supplier
• Operate efficient and effective processes
• Flow-chart • Streamline • Error-proof
• Build trust

The next step is for the team to streamline its process (see page 151). Processes that are cumbersome and needlessly complex are not only slow, they cause things to go wrong. Aim for simplicity. The more complicated a process, the greater the chance for error. With flow-chart in hand, the team should review its process to remove unnecessary steps and unclog bottlenecks. The team should look for activities duplicated elsewhere that could be eliminated from their process. It should search for needless control points which cause delays and mistakes because decisions are made by people who are not close to the customer or are not working with the process on a daily basis. Finally, the team should look at when things happen. Sometimes key activities which could be done at another time are performed at a peak period when people are very busy. This causes mistakes to be made and the fixing of those mistakes creates more work which further overloads the system.

After all, tangible product quality is merely the ticket to the dance. It does not mean you'll be queen of the ball.
Dr Earl Naumann,
Creating Customer Value

Processes work more effectively when staff are *empowered* to make decisions. Give each team the responsibility for operating its process efficiently and effectively. Efficient processes work quickly and produce minimum waste. Effective processes produce what customers need to be successful. Set targets in these areas, or better yet, get the team to set its own targets based on what its customers are saying. Require each team to monitor the performance of its process by collecting hard data and graphing the results. Give them the time and skills necessary to improve their process and reward them for improvements. Successful businesses are the result of staff working together in teams to operate efficient processes to make their customers successful. It is the job of management to create the environment where this can happen.

Successful businesses are the result of staff working together in teams to operate efficient processes to make their customers successful. It is the job of management to create the environment where this can happen.

Level Two

Providing Support Services

You must get the basics right because you rarely get a second chance these days. Still, the competition today and in the forseeable future will be mostly non-product competition. Products by themselves will not give you that competitive

There are just so many competent professionals to choose from, so many outstanding products and so many excellent services that you need to do more than have a good product or service to win.

advantage because they have nearly all reached the same level of reliability and sophistication. You can have the world's most unique product or service today and someone will have copied it by tomorrow. With so many outstanding products and so many excellent services available you need to compete by providing superior support services.

From the customer's perspective, support services and the basic product are virtually inseparable. A good example is the personal computer industry. According to consumer research reported in *Fortune* in December of 1995, although the quality of personal computers had improved over the previous

Seven Steps To Making Your Business Processes Effective

1. Organize your people into teams around their business processes.

2. Have each team flow chart its business process.

3. Ask each team to error-proof its process by:
   • finding commonly occurring mistakes;
   • identifying mistakes waiting to happen;
   • developing procedures to reduce the chances both of these could happen.

4. Ask each team to streamline its process by:
   • removing unnecessary steps;
   • unclogging bottlenecks;
   • simplifying the paperwork;
   • removing needless control points;
   • rescheduling some activities to avoid peak hour rushes;
   • identifying activities duplicated elsewhere.

5. Have each team measure how well its process operates
   • How long does it take to complete the process?
   • Where do the delays occur?
   • Where do things go wrong?

6. Have your teams review the performance of their process regularly

7. Give each team the time and skills to improve its process.

five years and prices had decreased significantly, customer satisfaction with PCs fell nearly 4 per cent in one year alone because of the poor performance of help-lines. Another example is the automobile industry. According to John Lindquist, a motor industry specialist with the Boston Consulting Group, the Toyota Corolla and the GM Geo Prizm are almost identical cars and sell for about the same price new. But the resale value of the Corolla is 18 per cent higher because of service provided by the Toyota dealer network. Toyota's support services sustained and even amplified the value of the car.

From your customer's perspective, support services and the basic product or service are virtually inseparable. Therefore, support services are a critical part of customer satisfaction.

Support services will increase the benefits you provide customers whether you offer them before the purchase, during the purchase transaction or after the purchase. They are the intangible things you do to reduce the costs customers pay and to make it possible for them to gain the most from your products and services. Support services include such things as providing education about your product or service and training in its use. It might be information you provide or advice you give. It could even be the use of technology or people to give people access to your company to place an order, arrange shipment or request assistance. If you are using Strategy 5, you will already have these support services in place.

Of course, the support services you offer must be important to the customer or you are wasting everyone's time and your money. I once read about a man who was offered state-funded counselling because he had been the victim of a crime. His lawnmower had been stolen. He declined the support, confessing to having only a passing fancy for the machine.

Since they flow from the culture of the organization, support services can be harder to copy than the features of a basic product or service. Some companies, such as Southwest Airlines and McDonalds (children's birthday parties) have been successful in using support services to make them unique. A few years ago, doing anything in the area of support services would have set you apart. If you provided after-sales service, if you had a toll-free telephone number, or if you provided free delivery you would stand out from the crowd. But not today. Customers expect the delivery to be free and to have comprehensive after-sales service including an 800 number.

The purpose of support services is to make it easier for your customers to do business with you and to derive the full benefits from using your products or services.

175

What Support Services Could You Provide?

Grocery Store
- free delivery to the elderly or the house-bound
- food tastings, cooking classes, menu planning

The Bank
- a welcome wagon for people new to town
- consultations to business on cash management
- consultations to families on budgeting

Restaurants
- reminders to people about special occasions
- fax the latest menu or weekly specials

Professional People
- baby-sitting services
- offer seminars

Service Station
- monthly account
- report of monthly or annual auto expenses
- collect your car to be fueled or serviced

Bookstore
- tell you about new books related to your interests
- send books on a trial basis
- hold book evenings with wine and cheese
- hold seminars for small businesses

Today, you should consider support services to be hygiene factors. You must do them well to succeed but no one will thank you if you do. Fail to provide them and you will lose sales.

Level Three

Give Them Something Extra

The third level is to provide additional benefits that your customers do not expect and are delighted to receive. This is where you give them something extra. Give your customers solutions to those problems they would love you to solve but can not reasonably expect that you will.

And, when you do, it knocks their socks off.

One man who understands the power of giving customers something extra is Jim Penman. Using delighters, Jim created a business which, you will remember, has become the largest lawn-mowing franchise in the world. When Jim mowed a lawn, he would look for something small he could do that would help his customer. Maybe he would remove some garden rubbish, weed a section of the garden or trim a bush. Then he would tell the customer what he had done but he would never charge them anything for it. The goodwill and loyalty he earned more than made up for the few dollars worth of his time he had given away. Through these simple acts, Penman increased the value he created for his customers because they got the impression they were "getting something for nothing". One or more benefits at no cost has got to add up to good value in anyone's eyes.

Give your customers solutions to those problems they would really like you to solve but cannot reasonably expect that you will. And, when you do, it knocks their socks off.

Not long ago I was on the receiving end of the "give them something extra" strategy so I know just how powerful it can be. My family and I arrived in Whakatane, a small coastal town in New Zealand, one winter's night and started looking for a motel. We tried a few but they either looked shabby or the front-desk service was lacklustre. Eventually, we found a place just off the main highway. I approached the empty office but before I could ring for the clerk he was there. I told him I needed a room for five. "We've only got one unit left," said the owner, "but I'm sure we can make it comfortable."

He was right. We did. An extra bed, some furniture rearranged; nothing was too much trouble. After everything was fixed up the owner asked us if we would like some hot blueberry muffins! That was the extra and at 9 p.m. on a cold winter's night that seemed like a very good idea. Needless to say, there was no charge for the additional bed or the muffins.

Sure, the customers benefit from all these extras but is there any benefit to this enterprising businessman? I asked him why his motel, located on a back street, was full on a mid-week night in the middle of winter. The town, after all, was not very big. The owner told me they are full nearly every week night because of all the travelling salespeople. "Why do they stay here when they have so many other choices?"

"I don't know. Maybe it's because we look after them. We put a couple of beers in the refrigerator in their rooms — that sort of thing."

Now, I cannot imagine a travelling salesperson being interested in a couple of free beers after a hard day talking to customers, can you?

Many other business people have discovered the power of giving their customers something extra. Canadian Tire, a major retail chain, began handing out its own money 36 years ago. For every dollar they spend, customers are given Canadian Tire money which can be used as cash at any of their stores. Harley Davidson owes its present existence to giving its customers something extra. A few years ago, the Rolls Royce of motorcycles was going broke. Among the changes management introduced was the Harley Owners Group (HOG). This exclusive club published a newsletter, operated a travel agency, organized local meetings and bike tours, provided free roadside assistance and much more. When a customer bought a Harley, they were given a free one-year membership to HOG. The club has proved to be so popular that it has become a major benefit of owning a Harley in the customers' eyes.

Some companies have discovered that giving people gifts or gift vouchers is good for business.

Some companies have discovered that giving people gifts or gift vouchers is good for business. Good Catalogue Co. in Portland, Oregon, a cataloguer with $16 million in sales in 1995, sends customers a $50 gift and a personalized letter every time they spend $250 or more on a single order. Of course, $50 is the retail price of the gift. It actually costs the company only $15. Within a few months of starting the programme response rates to mailings rose from 5 per cent to 25 per cent while the average order increased from $100 to $300. Similarly, a Florida restaurant chain gives its customers a $10 gift certificate for every $150 they spend. The programme has 15,000 members and accounts for 10 per cent of their sales. Frequent diners visit their restaurants between three and eight times a month as compared with one or two times for the average customer. They also spend more per visit. Small businesses are making this strategy work for them, too. Harrel Remodeling, a home renovation company in Menlo Park, California, gives each customer a gift certificate for dinner part way through a kitchen remodeling project.

A dentist I visited gives his customer a headpiece with built-

in headphones and screen so you can watch a video while he works. You know you are in trouble when he puts on a feature length movie! I once stayed at a motel where the owner offered to put a couple of loads of washing through her machine and brought them back clean, dried and neatly folded. No charge, of course. There are taxi drivers who provide coffee and soft drinks, newspapers and magazines, and a wide range of music to choose from. On one business trip when I was riding in a taxi I discovered that my cellphone was not working. The taxi driver gave me the name of a place in that city who could fix it and offered to take me there at no cost. Chris Zane, mentioned earlier as the the largest independent bicycle dealer in the New Haven, Connecticut area, charges nothing for things that cost less than a dollar.

Tourist attractions could benefit from giving their customers something extra. I once went to Arrowtown, an historic town in New Zealand's South Island which had been the site of a major gold rush in the last century. It is a well-known tourist spot. The trouble is, Arrowtown is just a small town — part pioneer village and part commercial centre. If the local community gave their customers something extra — a total experience instead of just a place to visit — they would add more value. They could, for example, close the streets to vehicular traffic, dress people in period costumes and have demonstrations and activities for people to enjoy. Probably no place

Many companies should start giving people something extra because it would enhance the value of their basic product or service and give them a competitive advantage.

does this better than Upper Canada Village, a pioneer village in Ontario, Canada. During the time it is open, from early spring to late autumn it is a working town from the 1800s. People farm, bake bread and teach school there the way it was done last century. Guests are drawn in to interact with the "residents" who play their parts very realistically. A day there is full of delighters.

Then there are those businesses who do the opposite of delighting their customers. Not only do they reduce the benefits at no extra cost, they increase the costs for no apparent benefit. Such as a motel that charged me $124 a night and then wanted to charge $2 per person to use the spa. Or another that charged $140 for a family unit and then charged extra to have the room serviced each day. But the business person who had the least understanding of value operated a restaurant my family and I once went to in Picton, New Zealand. After spending $17 on lunch, I asked for three glasses of water.

"That'll be 90 cents."

"You charge for water?"

"I'll have to use three glasses and walk to the tap."

Give me a break!

Using delighters is a powerful way to differentiate yourself from your competitors. Train your staff to look for opportunities to give your customers something extra.

Using delighters is a powerful way to differentiate yourself from your competitors.

Some time ago I delivered a series of one-day staff programmes for Ansett New Zealand, one of New Zealand's two domestic airlines. Ansett had come to New Zealand a few years earlier and blown the socks off Air New Zealand, which for years had had a monopoly. But as time went on, Air New Zealand got better and Ansett staff became complacent. Management thought the time had come to re-energize the company and get staff refocused on the customer. We called the day "Dare to Create Magic" and the main message was that our customers are our business and our planes are just like everyone else's, so let us be different by doing special things for our passengers. After people had gone through the programme, things began to happen. For example, one of the passenger agents found herself dealing with a fellow who was having one of those no good, awful, terrible, wish-I-was-in-Fiji days. He had a ticket for the wrong day, the flights were full — you know the story. After solving his problems the best she could, the passenger agent opened her purse and gave him the lottery ticket she had just bought for herself. "Let's hope your luck changes," she said. Now I do not know whether he won, but I bet Ansett did.

To work at this highest level of benefit creation, you must put yourself in your customer's shoes and learn to see the world through your customer's eyes (Strategy 3). Ask yourself:

- *What could I give my customers that no one else is giving them?*

- *What would surprise and delight me if I was a customer?*

Ask your customers, too. Watch them. Look for problems they have that you could solve at little cost to yourself but at great benefit to them. Remember those two good questions to ask your customers, no matter what business you are in, are:

What problems do you have satisfying your customers?

What problems do you have doing business with me?

Even the end-user has customers — usually their family and friends. If you can give your customers something extra that will help them to satisfy these important customers of theirs, you will have increased the benefits you offer.

Give your customers something extra and they will be delighted. They will tell a lot of other people about their experience, and most importantly, they *will* be back again. Their repeat business is your future security.

Now that you know what to do, the question is, "How are you going to make it happen?"

> *The trend today is inexorable: what customers want, and what they are increasingly able to get, is more-for-less... So no matter what business you are in, you must provide greater value, and not necessarily charge extra for it, to attract and retain customers.*
>
> Robert Tucker, *Win the Value Revolution*

Summary

• **To become second to none, you must give your customers more benefits at a lower cost.**

• **Many benefits are seen by consumers as simply hygiene factors.** Do them well and nobody notices. Do them poorly and you lose business.

• **There is a hierarchy of creating benefits.** You must do those at the lower levels before the higher level ones will work.

• **Level One is to create benefits through your basic product and service** but this is a hygiene factor. You must be a reliable supplier of a product or service that works just to stay in business. You become a reliable supplier by organizing your people into teams and then by giving them the responsibility, authority, time and skills to operate their business processes effectively and efficiently.

• **The second level is to provide support services** that make it easier for your customer to do business with you or to extract maximum benefit from your basic product or service. At one time, you could have gained a competitive advantage from providing support services but today they, too, are hygiene factors.

• **The third and most powerful level is to give your customers something extra.** Identify problems that your customers would love you to solve but do not seriously think you could. Then solve them — at no extra cost. Your customers will be delighted. They will want to become your business partner. And, they are likely to tell a lot of others how much benefit you have been to them. But most importantly, they will come back with repeat business.

How Are *You* Doing?

For each of your major products and services,
list the benefits.
First the hygiene factors:
- What are the benefits of your basic product
  or service?

- What are the benefits from your support services?

Then the delighters: What do you give that is extra?

Do you have the basics right? Are your processes effective?

- Have they been flow charted or documented?

- Have they been error-proofed?

- Have they been streamlined?

- Do you measure the performance of each process?

- Are the results reviewed and improvements made?

Which additional support services could you
provide?

What problems do your customers have that
they would just love you to solve for them?

What are your opportunities to give them something extra?

 Beginning The Journey

Making It Happen

If you have come this far, you have covered a lot of material. Now you have to make it happen. Follow these six steps and watch your business grow.

1. Begin With Your People

I work with a lot of enlightened senior managers and they tell me that their people are their most valuable asset. But people are not an asset, they are your organisation. Take them out of your company and what is going to happen? Not a lot.

The best place to begin then, is with your people. Transform your employees into business people. Employees think about their jobs. Business people think about creating value. Go back to Strategy 1, and get everyone in your organisation to understand that:

1. Your customers are paying only for value. They want results not activity.
2. Value = benefits – costs.
3. Value is subjective and variable. It exists only in the customer's mind.
4. Customers want benefits, not features. Benefits are features that solve the customer's problems.
5. Costs of time, effort and risk are more expensive than price for most customers.

2. Get Your Strategy Right

In this competitive business environment many companies are trying to compete on price and price alone. This is a mistake. Competing on only price will destroy your profitability and quite possibly damage your entire industry.

The alternative is to compete on value. Decide which value-based strategy is best for you but know that in this tough commercial climate you will probably be most successful if you try to increase the benefits you provide to your customers *and* reduce the costs they have to pay.

Once you have chosen your strategy, make sure everyone in the company knows what it is and why you have chosen it. Then make sure they understand it and what their role is in making it work.

3. Go Into The Marketplace

Business happens in the marketplace so your next step should be to go into the world of your customers. Make sure you take all your people with you so that they can see, understand and learn what you do. Learn to look at the world through your customers' eyes. Make sure that your business is working for the customer and that you are not, through your policies, procedures and blind spots, making your customers work for you.

Step outside your business and see what your customers see. Is your business easy to deal with? Are your staff friendly? Seek answers from your customers. If you listen, they will tell you everything you need to do to be successful. Focus your staff on the customers. Bring the paying customers into the workplace through meetings and video interviews. Require your staff to spend some time every week learning about their internal and external customers' needs and problems. Capture what you learn so that it can benefit future employees.

4. Make Your Customers Successful

Go beyond customer service and even customer satisfaction and become obsessed with making your customers successful. Understand your market and choose those customer segments you wish to target. Within that group, identify your key customers — those 20 per cent who bring you 80 per cent of your revenue. You do not have the resources to treat all your customers the same way, and you cannot become all things to all people in this age of niches and specialization. Build a relationship with your key customers and learn as much about them as you can. Talk to *their* customers to better understand what your customers have to do to succeed. Develop a business relationship with them that is based on the philosophy "if you win, I win". Aim to have not customers but partners. Better yet, turn your partners into advocates. It is the best and cheapest advertising you can get.

5. Reduce The Costs

Get your price within range of your competitors' and then work to reduce the other costs customers pay. Eliminate, reduce, or at least make clear, the costs of ownership. Reduce the costs of time and effort by streamlining your processes. Remove unnecessary steps and unclog bottlenecks. Remove the emotional costs people pay by becoming a reliable supplier. Most companies fail their customers, not through lack of concern about customer service, but because their processes are not robust. Error-proof your processes. Earn your customer's trust by being friendly, providing good information and by offering performance guarantees.

6. Give Them Something Extra

At the same time as you are working to reduce costs, increase the benefits you offer. Discover the problems your customers have and develop solutions. Both your basic products and services and your support services are hygiene factors. If they do not contain sufficient benefits no one will buy, but if they do, no one will really notice. To be second to none, you must give people something extra. Find those problems that your customers would love you to solve but cannot reasonably expect you to. Then solve them at little or no cost and knock their socks off.

Six Steps To Making It Happen

1. Begin with your people.

2. Get your strategy right.

3. Go into the marketplace.

4. Make your customers successful.

5. Reduce the costs.

6. Give them something extra.

# Epilogue

The Last Word

You paid money to get this book and you have spent time and effort reading it.

Did you receive value?

The answer to that, of course, depends on whether you believe you have gained any benefits and, if so, whether they have been sufficient to cover your costs.

From my point of view you have benefited greatly if you now understand:

1. That business is the art of creating value
2. That value = benefits – costs
3. That if you are competing to win you should increase the benefits in your products and services and decrease the costs
4. How to give your customers more benefits for less cost

But then, that is just my view and since you are the customer, it is your view that matters. So, the last word is really yours. I would really like to hear from you. Remove the last page of this book, jot down your comments, fold along the dotted lines, staple it shut and drop it in the post. It's that simple.

Meanwhile, I'll just say goodbye and good luck.

Dr Ian Brooks,
Auckland, New Zealand
September, 1997

Further Reading

Here is a suggested reading list for those interested in more information. It is not a comprehensive list. I have simply gathered together some interesting and often lesser known books that will add value to the way you run your business.

Keeping the Edge by Dick Schaaf. Penguin, New York, New York. 1995

The Popcorn Report by Faith Popcorn. HarperBusiness, New York, New York. 1991

Win the Value Revolution by Robert Tucker. Career Press, Franklin Lakes, New Jersey. 1995

Why Customers Don't Do What You Want Them To Do — And What To Do About It by Ferdinand Fournies. McGraw-Hill, New York, New York, 1994

How To Drive Your Competition Crazy by Guy Kawasaki. Herperion, New York, New York. 1995

Boom, Bust & Echo by David Foot. Macfarlane, Walter & Ross, Toronto, Ontario. 1996

How To Get New Business in 90 Days by Wendy Evans. Millenium Books, Newtown, NSW. 1993

Working Wisdom by John Dalla Costa. Stoddart, Toronto, Ontario. 1995

Hey, I'm The Customer by Ron Willingham. Prentice Hall, Englewood Cliffs, New Jersey. 1992

Competing On Value by Mack Hanan and Peter Karp, American Management Association, New York, New York. 1991

The Discipline of Market Leaders by Michael Treacy and Fred Wiersema. Adison-Wesley, Reading, Massachusetts. 1995

Built to Last by James Collins and Jerry Porras. HarperBusiness, New York, New York. 1994

Creating Customer Value by Earl Naumann. Thomson Executive Press, Cincinnati, Ohio. 1995

Index

Dear Ian

Dr Ian Brooks
Nahanni Business
PO Box 35 510
Browns Bay
Auckland 10

Cut along dotted line